"This guide is candid and well-written... intended less to convert than to interest and stimulate."
—Western Publisher

"A rich and full book... too positive to resist."
—Mothering

"Allen succeeds in conveying a cheerful, conversational tone, and the reader is made to feel good about the work at hand (self-improvement). Material that less-skillful hands might have obscured in cultish vocabulary is made accessible... Allen makes it clear he won't demand that you give up meat, TV, or alcohol, only that you take a leap. A fun leap, but a leap nevertheless... A person seeking change in his approach to life would do himself a service by taking a look at *Tantra for the West.*"
—San Diego Tribune

"An example of how Eastern wisdom which evolved centuries ago has a contemporary meaning for the problems of today... a splendid interface of east and west, old and new, esoteric and practical."
—Stanley Krippner, Ph.D.,
Faculty Chair, Humanistic Psychology Institute,
co-editor of Future Science,
author of *Human Possibilities*

"*Tantra for the West* conveys clearly the awesome creative power available to our deep intuitive nature. Every chapter demonstrates wisdom and insight... and is alive and obviously grounded in Marcus Allen's personal experience."
—Ariel Kent, Ph.D.,
Founding Director, San Francisco Institute for
Transformational Psychologies

"A clear, simple style... congruent with its message."
—Virginia Satir, M.A., D.S.S.,
author of *Peoplemaking, Making Contact,*
and *Self Esteem*

"The word 'prosper' in its root means 'wholeness'. That is what this book is all about: how to experience wholeness in every phase of one's life. It is filled with a practical mysticism from which we can all benefit as we enter this New Age of enlightenment."

—Rev. Catherine Ponder,
Unity Church Worldwide

"This is a valuable tool for people in their lives for better understanding of themselves."

—Carol Augustus,
co-founder and President of Actualizations

"Written in a practical and delightfully readable style, *Tantra for the West* dispels many of the myths about what tantra is and is not."

—Susan Campbell, Ph.D.,
author of *The Couples Journey*, and
Barry McWaters, Ph.D.,
author of *Conscious Evolution*

Tantra for the West—A Guide to Personal Freedom is a most honest book, which shows people of all backgrounds how to appreciate life more and how to enjoy being alive and becoming more whole. Beautiful!"

—Elisabeth Kubler-Ross, M.D.

"Here is the best of the East in clear and simple terms for everyone who wants to live a life full of spirit in the West!"

—Bruce and Genny Davis,
authors of *The Lovers' Book* and
The Magical Child Within

"The West is increasingly enriched by those writers who have a gift for cross-cultural bridging. Marcus Allen is such a writer."

—Marilyn Ferguson,
author of *The Aquarian Conspiracy*

MARCUS ALLEN

TANTRA
FOR THE WEST

A GUIDE TO PERSONAL FREEDOM

Whatever Publishing
San Rafael, California

Published by
Whatever Publishing, Inc.
58 Paul Drive
San Rafael, CA 94903

87   88   89   90   11   10   9   8

Cover by
Kathleen Vande Kieft

Library of Congress Cataloging in Publication Data

Allen, Mark, 1946-
    Tantra for the West.

    Bibliography: p. 231
    1. Spiritual life.   2. Religious life (Tantric
Buddhism)   I. Title
BL624.A45   294.3'444   80-316
ISBN 0-931432-06-5

Dedicated with love to
Shakti Gawain
and
Sharon Scandur,
for you've each
in your own way
taught me about tantra

Contents

Preface   9
    By Jeffrey Mishlove

Introduction   10

  I **Opening**   13
    Tantra defined

 II **The brilliant concept of tantra**   17
    Three different paths. Confronting negative
    feelings. A tantric practice. A message to
    myself.

III **Affirmations**   31
    The power of affirmations. The act of
    creation. The power of your words. How to do
    affirmations. Affirmations in meditation.
    Writing affirmations. A common error. Have
    patience. The law of karma. Easily and
    effortlessly.

IV Relationships   **49**
Tantric relationships. What do you want? The
inner planes. The outer plane. Negotiation.
Dealing with conflict. Jealousy, fear, and
anger. Sharings. A key to fulfilling
relationships.

V Sex   **69**
Some questions for you to answer. Trust
yourself! Sexual energy. Tantric sex. One
beautiful way to make love. Sustaining sexual
energy. To come or not to come? Making love.
An exercise. A meditation for love-making.

VI Being alone   **87**
Self-examination. The self-questioning
process. A meditation on being alone.

VII Work   **91**
Look at your beliefs. Your highest purpose.
Your ideal. A meditation to create your perfect
work. Enjoy your work.

VIII Money   **101**
Limiting beliefs. A creative meditation for
money. Creating abundance. The ten-percent
plan. To sum it up.

IX Creativity   **111**
Unlocking your creative genius. Let go of the
judge. A 15-minute exercise. A tantric
musician. A meditation for opening up
creativity. Some good advice.

X Food and drink   **123**
A tantric experiment. You are not what you
eat. A meditation.

XI Meditation and yoga 129
The benefits. The pitfalls. Meditation.
Silence. The active forms of meditation. Pillar
of light. Opening up your energy centers.
Creative meditations. A meditation on our
three bodies. Be with yourself. Closing the
gates. Mantra. Yoga and tantra. Hatha yoga.
Kum nye. Free form yoga. The Way is Infinite.

XII Aging and healing 157
A youthful observation. The aging process.
Think yourself thin. An exercise. Create a
young, beautiful body. A face exercise. The
principles of healing. Keep growing.

XIII Politics 169
Your personal power. The deep meaning of
karma. New Age politics.

XIV Enlightenment 177

XV Freedom 183
To sum it up — a final exercise. Shattering
models. You are free if you affirm yourself to
be.

Appendix A: Tantra in the East: A brief, unscholarly
history of Tibetan (Tantric) Buddhism 189
The historical roots of tantra. The Nyingma
School. The Gelugpa School. The Kargyud
School. The Sakya School. A story. Tibetan
Buddhism today. Tantra in the West.

Appendix B: Reflections 212

Acknowledgements 226

Bibliography 231

Preface

Tantra has been pulled up by the roots from its rocky Tibetan soil and transplanted in the lush gardens of America. This book, the fruit of a garden of unique experiences cultivated by Marcus Allen, promises to quicken the reverberation of sacred unity within our Western souls. One need only breathe deeply to appreciate the musky blend of both subtle and powerful aromas within — the fragrance of the fresh wind of freedom — and the new American tantric experience begins, in a cross-cultural context only dimly imagined by the ancient masters.

Jeffrey Mishlove
author of *Roots of Consciousness*

Introduction

Every one of us is on a journey, a journey of our own personal evolution. It is the nature of all life forms to grow and evolve, and we are no exception. Each one of us has our own unique style — some of us are very disciplined, and some of us have no concept of or interest in discipline, and would rather drink beer and watch TV.

My intention in writing this book is to share with you a perspective which hopefully is supportive and eye-opening... and which can give you some deep, meaningful understanding and some very practical tools to assist in your own personal growth, regardless of the way you choose to live your life.

The form of this book is often concise and intentionally brief, covering a lot of ground. It is suggestive rather than explanatory. Its intent is to show you that the answers are within you — not anywhere else, in any book or anyone else's teachings.

Within your everyday thoughts and feelings, within your way of life, within your fantasies and your dreams are the keys to your own true personal freedom.

Please read this book slowly. Don't move through it once, rapidly, intellectually, and think you have absorbed it all. Take your time . . . take time to do some of the exercises . . . take time to pause at the dots, and take a breath . . . and enjoy!

Who seeks for heaven alone
to save his soul
May keep the path,
but will not reach the goal
While they who walk in love
may wander far
Yet God will bring them
where the blessed are.

— Henry Van Dyke
The Other Wise Man

I

Opening

Tantra for the West – A guide to personal freedom . . . .

The first book I wrote about *tantra* didn't use the word even once. I felt that because tantra is so misunderstood, so badly mistranslated in the West, it was better not to use the term at all and to avoid the confusion of trying to redefine it. So I chose the word 'reunion' instead, and called the book *Reunion: Tools for Transformation.*

But the concept embodied in the word *tantra* is so brilliant, and so useful to open minds in the West at this time, that I find myself drawn to using it again and again . . . and I find myself writing about it once again. For tantra, clearly understood and practiced, can be the most effective key to personal freedom available to us.

Tantra defined

Tantra is not just 'the yoga of sex', as is so often

believed — it is the yoga of *everything*. And 'yoga' means 'union'. So, a good way to define tantra is 'the union of everything', or 'the unity of every moment'. Another very good way to define tantra is: *the awareness that creates complete personal freedom within every moment of our daily lives, rejecting nothing.*

Tantra is a path, a means, to personal freedom. What is personal freedom? That is entirely up to you to discover and create for yourself, for freedom is being free to be yourself.

Tantra is wide open, with infinite possibilities — like life is, and like you are. Tantra includes sex, yet it includes everything else, too — every moment of your life. Every moment is sacred, every moment is to be enjoyed and/or used as a *teaching* — a piece of valuable instruction, a message — for you to grow by.

Everything you are doing, have done, and will do are part of your practice of tantra, for tantra uses every moment as a vehicle to freedom. Through an awareness of tantra, we discover the unique perfection of every moment of our lives.

You don't have to believe this — you don't have to believe anything which follows. Simply read with an open mind, try some of the exercises, and see what happens. This book is meant to be worked with and played with, rather than just read straight through. It contains powerful tools to help you attain happiness, freedom, love, abundance, power, enjoyment, fulfillment — *whatever your heart desires*. But the tools must be applied, not just read. Understanding intellectually is a very different thing from experiencing deeply, with your whole being. Intellectual understanding has no effect at all on the quality of your daily life, while experiencing deeply can work miracles.

You can work miracles in your life by investigating the principles and using the techniques which follow — if you wish. All you have to do is open up to them. It is up to you.

Within our darkest moments,
our brightest treasures can be found.

II

The Brilliant Concept of Tantra

The concept and vast body of teachings embraced by the word *tantra* is far more ancient than any scholar or historian could ever trace. The word itself comes from the ancient Sanskrit root word meaning *to weave*. Tantra is the stuff of life, the unique fabric of our lives which we have woven over the years.

Tantra has come to us through two vast, multi-faceted traditions: Hindu tantra and Buddhist tantra. Both originated in India, in all likelihood, although Buddhist tantra comes to us through the Tibetan culture, because Buddhism disappeared in India about 1200 years ago. (See Appendix A: Tantra in the East, for more historical details.)

Although every form of tantra is unique and different, some important generalizations can be made about all tantra:

Tantra is a way of life which involves acceptance, not rejection, of all of life. It does not reject anyone or any particular 'spiritual path' or psychological area of study. It embraces the whole of life. Everything has its own perfect reason for being.

Tantra shows that within every moment of our lives — within every feeling and thought and activity — is contained deep and powerful truths which, if examined in a clear light, can lead to true personal freedom in a very short time.

Tantra teaches respect for the individual, and recognizes that every individual must evolve in his or her own way. There is no pat system which will work for everyone. There is only endless evolution, which we are involved in whether we are conscious of it or not. Simply becoming conscious of this process is the most important thing we can do to speed up the process, and move into a state of being where we are happy and free.

The Western world is now ripe for the ideas and practices of tantra. Westerners are often too individualistic and too worldly-wise to accept most forms of Eastern thought and practice, because they contain a great many of the cultural trappings of India. While India has been a fertile source of great philosophy and spiritual truths, the country is still very much influenced by the Victorian beliefs and attitudes which were deeply instilled during the British rule. As a result, many of the spiritual and philosophical traditions of the East seem to encourage Westerners to go without sex, meat, alcohol, coffee or any other 'impure' foods, to live a life of rigorous discipline, and to reject a great part of the culture, heritage, and lifestyles of the West.

A study of the history of tantra reveals that its power, its ability to adapt so successfully to other cultures, relies on the fact that it does not reject anything of the culture to which it has been introduced. We don't have to give up sex and meat and TV in order to achieve freedom and happiness. This is the effectiveness and power of tantra. We can create our lives exactly as we want them to be.

Three different paths

There is a season for everything, a time for every path. The path of tantra is not for everyone, by any means — only for those who are ready to take a leap.

A Tibetan *lama*, a fascinating teacher who is now in America, told me the following short parable. It is a traditional Tibetan story, and it places the different paths of different people into a simple, clear perspective while defining tantra beautifully.

There is a path going through the woods. A dense patch of poisonous plants is growing by the side of the path and, at one point, it totally engulfs the path.

A monk — with shaved head, robes, and begging bowl — comes up the path. The monk sees the poison, and immediately turns around and heads the other way.

Then the Bodhisattva — the spiritual seeker, working for the enlightenment of all beings — comes up the path. Seeing no way around the poisonous plants, the seeker courageously and hurriedly plows directly through them, and keeps moving on up the path.

Finally, a tantric yogi comes wandering up the path. This person has no outward signs

*of spiritual interest, unlike the monk or the
Bodhisattva. The follower of tantra sees the
poison, and plunges directly into the center of
it, even though it apparently takes him or her
off the path . . . .*

The key to understanding this story is the key
which enables us to discover the value of tantra in our
lives: the key is that the poisonous plants represent the
so-called 'negative' or 'separating' emotions — anger,
fear, greed, jealousy, etc. (Interestingly enough, the
Tibetan word for 'poison' is the same as the word for
'negative emotion'.) This little story presents a clear
picture of three alternative reactions to our own feelings: we can run from them, we can plow through them
as quickly as possible, or we can jump into them and
experience them fully.

None of these three choices are any better than the
others — each person in the parable just did what they
had to do, and each must be respected. It is perfect for
monks in some traditions to withdraw from the world,
and to attempt to ignore or even annihilate their feelings. And it is perfect for some people to avoid talking of
negative feelings or death, and to "put on a happy face"
— we all do simply what we need to do on the level of
evolution we have attained. But it is useful to be aware
that these people are being motivated by fear, and are
not examining their feelings.

It is perfect for the spiritual seekers to plow through
their negative feelings quickly and continue up the path
of their work in the world. Some people consider their
negative feelings as things to be dealt with as quickly as
possible, in order to get into a more loving, helpful
frame of mind.

Are the 'tantric yogis' more evolved or less evolved as they plunge into the 'poison' of their own negative or separating feelings? It is impossible to say. But one thing is known for sure — using this method, they will evolve faster, by leaps and bounds, than with the slower methods, which avoid or at least try to minimize negative feelings. For one of the most important things to realize about our so-called 'negative' feelings is that until they are openly looked at, clearly understood, and dealt with effectively, they retain their power, and keep resurfacing over and over again.

The path of tantra is the path of leaping into the fire of our feelings. This is ultimately a path of tremendous power and true freedom. It means going with the spontaneous expression of our feelings — something which children are natural masters of, before it is educated out of them, before they are taught to give up their freedom and sit for six hours a day in a classroom, exercising their rational minds, burying their intuitive visions, and suppressing their feelings.

Confronting negative feelings

The practice of tantra involves every moment of our lives. It involves an acceptance of, and a willingness to deal with, *all* of our thoughts, feelings, and actions — both the so-called positive feelings and the so-called negative feelings.

For years, while I was deeply exploring many of the studies which culminated in this book, I was not allowing myself to express my 'negative' feelings. I felt it was necessary for me to be positive, accepting, 'conscious' all the time, never blaming or criticizing anyone. For several years, in fact, I truly believed that I had gone beyond the 'lower, negative' feelings in which I saw many others still trapped. A deep yet subtle change came over me — one so subtle that I didn't realize it until I had gone beyond it: by not allowing myself to feel my so-called negative feelings, I was cutting myself off from my most positive feelings as well. I went for a long time without allowing myself to be angry or depressed, but I did so by narrowing my whole range of acceptable feelings. I could stay consistently content and somewhat peaceful, and be happy a lot of the time, but I didn't really experience any deep joy, or overwhelming love, or high enthusiasm. My life had become bland and limited; by not allowing myself to feel my anger and fear, I was not allowing myself to truly feel my love and joy.

As soon as I finally gave myself permission to have so-called 'negative' feelings again, to 'plunge into the poison', all kinds of positive feelings surfaced as well. My whole range of emotional experience broadened. And life became much richer and more satisfying. The practice of tantra involves letting yourself feel *everything*, regardless of whether you or someone else may judge it as positive or negative.

By confronting our own negative feelings, we are plunging into the heart of tantric practice. And that's what I'm inviting you to do — right now, right at the start of this book, the start of your journey into tantra. I can sense some of you thinking, "Wait a minute! I thought tantra was entirely different. I thought it was going to be fun and exciting!" Well, I can promise you that it will become fun and exciting — but we have some homework to do first, some inner work, which is given to us whenever we create a situation which is *not* fun or exciting.

Many others have said that they don't dare confront their negative feelings, because they would hurt somebody, or destroy something which they would later regret. One man at a workshop I gave once went so far as to say that, if he plunged into his feelings, he might go and rape hundreds of women and kill hundreds of men! The one thing these people don't realize is that there are *skillful* ways to get into your feelings — ways which don't hurt others, or yourself. Many of the exercises which follow deal with these methods.

Most people are afraid of their anger, and this keeps them from really confronting and expressing it. But then they end up carrying this anger around with them for years and years. It ends up damaging their bodies, and often their relationships, because it comes out in all kinds of covert ways, such as irritation, nervousness, tension, and periods of deadened silence.

By expressing that anger, you can let go of it. But you don't have to attack anyone else to express it. Two of the best methods I know of to get something off your chest are: (1) let yourself yell and rant and rave and condemn and say all kinds of terrible things when you're driving in your car alone, and (2) go into your room alone and put a pillow on your bed and pretend that pillow is the person you are angry at. Then proceed to pound it, with as much physical energy as you can put into it. Pound it to shreds, if necessary, to blow off your steam.

You'll notice that, if you allow yourself to really act out your anger in these ways which don't hurt anyone, afterwards you'll feel much better, lighter, more relieved. Most important, you've let go of that anger, and you aren't carrying it around with you anymore.

If it comes up again, do it again, and again if neces-

sary. But you'll soon work it out, and it won't come up
again.

A very important thing to become aware of,
whenever you're in an 'unpleasant' place, or confronting a 'negative' emotion, is this: It is not necessarily the
situation itself, or the emotion itself, which is causing
you your problem — it is your own rejection of the
situation, and your own rejection of your feelings,
which is causing the problem to be far worse than it
would be otherwise.

Don't reject your feelings. Instead, be with them,
respect them, examine them. Look closely, and gently,
at them. Simply look at what you're telling yourself,
and see the thoughts which are going through your
mind. Look at them honestly, openly, and as objectively
as possible.

These moments are your finest sources of instruction. Your own feelings are a storehouse of wisdom, if
you embrace them, and look closely at them.

You may be wondering what kind of wisdom can
come from being angry or jealous or guilty. Look at it
this way: there's a reason why you are feeling those
things, often a very simple reason. But, when you're
caught up in those emotions, you can't see why you're
creating them. If you take some time to ask yourself
why you're feeling the way you are, you can begin to
learn things about yourself that you've never quite seen
so clearly. That knowledge alone can produce some very
good changes in your way of life — changes which free
you in a great many ways. The following exercise, 'a
tantric practice', gives you very specific instructions in
how to do this.

This may seem like a time of indecision . . . or

regret... or pain... or anger. But look again — don't reject these feelings, but embrace them instead. Welcome them, even act them out (as long as you don't hurt anyone else)! Discover what you're telling yourself, even if it sounds stupid, or violent, or unloving, or negative. By simply exposing these hidden feelings to view, you are shining the light of your understanding upon them, and you are seeing exactly where you are limiting yourself. Many so-called negative feelings will simply dissolve when looked at in the clear light of an accepting, open mind. Others will need more powerful techniques, which we will explore in later chapters.

It is important to see that every so-called negative feeling can be the beginning of the understanding which leads to true freedom. Every feeling contains within it an opportunity for growth — if you can allow yourself to plunge into it, and discover what it is.

If Buddha — the historical Buddha who revolutionized religion and philosophy in India 2500 years ago — hadn't gone into a period of deep upset and anxiety, propelled into despair by fear of sickness, old age, and death, he never would have begun his many years of searching and examining. And he never would have become a Buddha, a 'Fully Awakened One'.

Within our darkest moments, our brightest treasures can be found.

A tantric practice

Here is the first tantric practice given in this book. To many, it may come as a surprise — for it does not deal with the usual things associated with 'tantric practices'. But you will see that it is truly a tantric practice in the broadest, most meaningful use of the word. It is designed to give you insight into yourself.

This is a four-step exercise to be done when you are feeling uncomfortable, emotionally upset, pressuring yourself to make a decision, or any time you wish to get more deeply in touch with yourself. Remember that the very state of mind you are in at any given moment is the perfect teaching for you at that moment. This exercise can help to clarify the teaching which is within every one of your feelings. It can help you break through the feelings which seem to be controlling you, and give you the power to master your own feelings, and yourself. Don't skip over any of these steps — especially the ones which seem insignificant. Do them all:

(1) Ask yourself a question which confronts or examines the feelings you are experiencing. It could be, "What am I telling myself right now?" or "What is the truth for me about _____?" or even "What am I feeling right now?"

(2) Answer yourself with the very first words that come into your mind, without censoring anything.

(3) Acknowledge yourself, each time you answer, by saying "Thank you!" to yourself for sharing these feelings. Then repeat these steps again, and again — until you finally arrive at an answer which sheds the light of clear understanding upon your situation. You'll know when it happens because you will suddenly feel better, clearer, more aware of your feelings and attitudes, and more aware of your options.

(4) Share your discovery with someone

*else, within a day or two. Even if you have to
call or write somebody, it is important to
share your feelings and your insight with
someone you are close to. This finalizes the
whole process.*

This exercise is so simple — yet so powerful! It
brings to the surface all the feelings which we are experiencing on deep levels that we don't allow ourselves
to examine consciously because they're not 'nice' feelings. Once they surface, and once we accept them, they
lose their power. It is important not to reject these
feelings — by rejecting them, we are giving them power
to run our lives. The reason that this happens is that
we're conditioned into a false belief that these feelings
are real and powerful, when in reality they have no
power to affect us. Accept them, say "Thank you!" to
yourself for expressing them, and look at them in the
light of your conscious mind. The simple act of accepting our feelings works miracles. The simple steps of this
exercise allow us to get down to the truth of what we're
feeling.

Try this exercise the next time you're upset, or
when you are dealing with a problem that seems impossible to resolve. Keep doing it until you get down to the
root of the problem, and you'll find yourself dissolving
the problem at its roots. And you'll find the true meaning of the word *tantra*.

A message to myself

Don't reject the sadness
Don't reject the sorrow
Don't reject the suffering
And the pain

Blessed are these things
For through them we grow
Into true understanding
Of our way

Positive affirmations have the greatest power in the universe behind them: the power of truth.

III

Affirmations

The exercise in the previous chapter simply involved confronting and accepting your emotional states, openly and honestly. In so many cases, that's all that is necessary to do. In other cases, we have to use other methods to teach ourselves to be free. Affirmations are one of the simplest and most powerful things we can do to change the quality of our lives, and to create the things we want.

The power of affirmations

The power of affirmations can be stated very simply: Affirmations are the force of creation. For

"In the beginning was the word...."
(John 1:1)

To affirm means 'to make firm'. There is very little

mystery about how and why affirmations work, once the principle is understood. An affirmation is simply a spoken declaration, in the present tense, which creates a desired reality.

We have been giving ourselves affirmations all our lives. And others have been giving us affirmations all our lives. The only problem has been that we have not been consciously aware of the process and power of affirmations, and so we have affirmed a lot of things which we could do better without.

Anything you say or think to yourself is an affirmation. Anything anyone else says to you is an affirmation, if you accept it. Our subconscious minds accept it all — whether for better or worse. Most of use grew up in environments which weren't totally supportive; most of us had parents, families, friends, and other peers who gave us a lot of terrible affirmations which were destructive to our self-image. Children often tell each other that they're stupid or ugly or unable to do something. Brothers or sisters often say unflattering things to each other. These are unfortunate, negative affirmations.

Most people are still carrying with them, in their basic core beliefs, the non-supportive things which their parents, teachers, friends, and families told them when they were so young that they didn't have the awareness to question or ignore. And these affirmations have an especially powerful effect when there's a strong emotion behind them — those moments when Mommy is deeply upset, and yells, "You never do anything for me!" give the child a deep affirmation of his or her own selfishness and worthlessness.

It's no wonder that people have affirmed themselves into neurosis, poverty, selfishness, unattractiveness, sickness, weak and limited self-images, etc. Fortunately, affirmations are so powerful that a few minutes of conscious, deep, positive ones repeated daily for a few weeks can undo years of unconscious, deep, negative ones. This is especially true because the positive affirmations have the greatest power in the universe behind them: the power of truth. Because the truth is that you *are* a free being — you are not limited or restricted. And your life is worthwhile. And you are a good person — not a bad one. And you are really loving — even though that love may be buried under years of unexpressed anger and guilt and frustration.

Affirm what you know to be true in your heart, and you will create that reality. Affirm that you are free, and strong, and attractive, and prosperous, and loving — and you will find, often in a remarkably short time, that your outer world will begin to change as a reflection of your changing inner consciousness.

The act of creation

To understand how an affirmation has the power to create something, we must first understand how creation works. A great many different mythologies, mystical traditions, scientific studies, and religions have investigated the mysteries of creation. Many of these have come up with similar findings. I feel that the *Kabbala* — so-called 'esoteric' Judaism — expresses it very clearly and simply. Those who have studied other traditions will see many similarities.

To study the Kabbala is to study the 'Tree of Life'. All things are contained within the Tree of Life. The creation of the Tree of Life reflects the mysteries of all creation. And the study of the Tree of Life explains the mysteries of ourselves, for we are a microcosm, mirroring the vast macrocosm: 'As above, so below'.

The Tree of Life begins within emptiness, within the vast, shining void of space. Then it begins as a very subtle 'spiritual impulse' — the impulse to create. Then this very subtle spiritual impulse becomes something more tangible: a *thought*, a clearer, more definite impulse to create something. Once the impulse has become a thought, it gains momentum and becomes a *feeling*, an emotional impulse. This feeling, supported by a sustained thought, *soon becomes manifest in physical form*, as an object we can experience with our senses.

The way in which the Tree of Life is formed reflects the way in which everything in our lives is created. Everything has gone through this cycle: it is first a spiritual impulse, then a thought, then a feeling, then it becomes a physical manifestation. Everything we have created in our lives was first a thought, and then a feeling. Anything we consistently hold in our minds to be true or real will become true or real in our physical universe.

This explains why affirmations are so powerful — and why they aren't so mysterious. Affirmations are our very thoughts themselves, supported by our emotions. We are saying affirmations all the time — whether consciously or unconsciously. The universe always says 'yes' to our affirmations, always supports them, because *we* are the universe, *we* are the Tree of Life, and we are creating our own reality, through our thoughts and feelings and spiritual impulses.

The power of your words

Through our words and the thoughts behind them, we are continually giving our bodies operating instructions. By being *observant*, we can become aware of this process.

As we have seen, everything, before it is created on the physical plane, is at first a thought, then a feeling. Before we can build a house, there must be a blueprint for it, a design, an *idea*. Words are creative ideas spoken, made manifest into the world.

Many people are unconscious of this — and they are so often saying things like, "This is really making me sick," or "This job is killing me," or "He's a pain in the neck," or "This is driving me crazy," or "I can't do it." These words are affirmations, just like any other words. No wonder these people are getting sick, dying too young at jobs they hate, getting headaches, going crazy, and failing in life.

Look at your life — clearly and honestly. You'll see what you have been affirming to yourself. Most of us have created a lot of things that we would prefer to do without. It is time to affirm, to create something better for yourself.

How to do affirmations

Every thought and every word — positive or negative — is an affirmation, and is creating the reality of the affirmation. The simplest way to do affirmations consciously is just to say them to yourself, either out loud or silently, whenever you feel like it. Especially say them to counteract any negative thoughts or words you find yourself thinking or saying. This is not a tool for repression — allow yourself to have any thoughts and feelings you have — don't reject them — and yet, give yourself the time and energy to affirm a more desirable reality after you have experienced and explored your so-called 'negative' feelings.

For example, if you find yourself thinking, "This job is making me sick," look at what you're thinking, and see if that's something you really want to create for yourself. If it isn't, affirm to yourself, out loud or silently, and with emotion, "I am strong and healthy when I do my work," or "I am eternally strong, healthy, and young," or something which feels good to you. Say it repeatedly, if necessary, and say it with emotion, until it feels like it has sunk in. By just becoming more aware of what you are saying and what you are thinking, you will find that you have plenty of material to deal with. Notice the things that aren't working in your life, and find affirmations to correct the situations.

Of course, your feelings about your job may be a very valid reason for you to find another, healthier job. But if you choose for the present to remain in the same situation, create the most positive thoughts you can about it.

Make the affirmations in the present tense — even if it seems unrealistic. Don't affirm, "I *am going to create* abundance in my life," because the results will always be waiting to happen in the future. Instead, suspend your current beliefs for a moment, and affirm, "I now have abundance in my life!" — and you'll soon find that it is true. How soon your abundance will come depends on how strongly your affirmation is repeated, and whether or not you are affirming the opposite on deeper levels of your consciousness (your subconscious negative beliefs).

Affirmations in meditation

Another powerful way to do affirmations is in the relaxed state of mind and body which is often called 'meditation'. By all means, find some time to meditate — even just five minutes in the morning will bring results within a week or two. The following exercise is relaxing, energizing, and healthful, as well as being the most powerful way to deeply absorb affirmations. It is the most effective way to create anything you wish.

Just sit or lie comfortably. Take a few deep cleansing breaths — even take a few minutes to breathe deeply, if you get into it. Deep breathing is one of the best possible things we can do for our minds, bodies, and spirits.

Close your eyes, take a deep breath and affirm, silently to yourself as you exhale, "My body is now relaxing." Take another breath and affirm, as you exhale, "My mind is now relaxing." Take one last deep breath and affirm, as you exhale, "I am now letting everything go."

Then choose any affirmation — any instructions you want to give your body and mind, anything you wish to create. See it happening here and now as you say your affirmations. If excitement and enthusiasm arises to support the affirmation, all the better – the stronger the feeling, the sooner the reality you wish to create manifests.

Say each one repeatedly, until it feels good to you. Try these, and see how they feel:

"I am deeply relaxed . . . .
"I am strong and healthy . . . .
"I am open, I am free . . . ."

Feel yourself being relaxed. See yourself strong and healthy. Feel yourself open and free.

Choose any other affirmations you wish to work on, and repeat them, many times, until you feel sure that your subconscious has unquestionably gotten the message. Picture yourself as having completely fulfilled the affirmation.

Enjoy yourself — don't work too hard at this. Have fun with your creative imagination.

Take a final, deep breath at the end of your meditative affirmations, and affirm,

"This, or something better, is now manifesting, for the highest good of all! So be it! So it is!"

Now return to your waking day, fully relaxed and refreshed, recharged, able to effortlessly accomplish whatever you want.

The more energy you put into your affirmations, the sooner you will experience results. Imagine yourself easily and effortlessly becoming what you are affirming. Don't worry if you can't exactly 'visualize' it in your mind's eye — just feel it, imagine it. By doing so, you are creating that reality in your thoughts, and in your emotions. Soon a vast, deep reservoir of power in you — the power of your subconscious mind, your connection with the infinite — will bring about in physical reality what you are affirming.

Writing affirmations

The measure of an affirmation's success is whether or not it soon manifests in your world. You should be able to manifest almost anything you are affirming within 21 days. There are some exceptions to this, if the project is vast or complicated, or the goal is distant. But the results should become clearly evident to you in a short time. You should be able to feel the change. If the results aren't happening, it is only because you are affirming something else on deeper, perhaps less conscious, levels which is creating something contradictory to what you are affirming consciously.

If you're repeating to yourself, for example,

"My connection with infinite intelligence
is yielding me a vast personal fortune."

every day, with emotion, and after three weeks you are still broke, then you have to find out what else you have been telling yourself that is creating a contradictory reality. Writing affirmations and their responses is the best way to do this.

Take a notebook. On one page, write "Affirmations" across the top. On the next page, write "Thank you!" across the top. Then begin writing your affirmation on the page headed "Affirmations." Put your attention into it; pour your feeling into it. You want to be self-sufficient, or beautiful, or whatever — and the truth of the matter is that *you deserve it*, so you might as well create it for yourself.

Keep on writing the same affirmation, and keep putting your full attention on it. Soon you will probably notice some kind of inner resistance popping up —

some words you are telling yourself (affirming to yourself) on deep levels. Whatever they are, write them down on your "Thank you!" page. On this page, you are encouraged to voice all of your reactions to your affirmation.

Say you're writing, for example, *"My connection with infinite intelligence...,"* and you find yourself thinking, "What connection? I'm a blundering idiot!" Immediately turn to your "Thank you!" page and write those words. It is called your "Thank you" page because, as you write those words, you want to mentally thank yourself for sharing them with you (this may sound artificial or strange, perhaps, but it *works*). Then go back to writing your affirmation *"... is yielding me a vast personal fortune."* Then you may find yourself thinking, "A vast personal fortune? I could never handle it!" — so write that down too on your "Thank you" page. Then go back and write your affirmation again. And so on.

After writing your affirmation 10 or 20 times, you may have 10 or 20 or 30 comments on your "Thank you!" page. Look at them carefully — these are the things you are affirming to yourself on deeper levels which are creating your present reality. Sometimes it is enough just to look at them and see how foolish they are, and how they are not really true for you. Sometimes these negative affirmations dissolve as soon as you look at them. At other times, you may have to create new affirmations for yourself that are especially designed to counteract what you have been telling yourself. In the example above, where you found that you were thinking you could never handle a vast personal fortune, you may want to affirm something like, *"I am capable of handling a vast personal fortune easily and skillfully"* —

or, if that is too confronting, lower the gradient for yourself and affirm, *"I am capable of skillfully handling my finances."*

Do this daily, if necessary. Break down your resistances with more affirmations. That is all that is necessary to do. When you finally get to the core of your resistance — to the "biggie" which you are holding onto, the one terrible thing about yourself that you haven't dared to admit even to yourself — when you finally find yourself writing it out on your "Thank you!" sheet, you'll feel something releasing in you. Then find the affirmation which deals with it directly and releases it for all time from your consciousness. You'll find yourself feeling wonderful (literally — *wonder full*). Now you are coming into your own power. Now you're not limiting yourself any more. You're free to be who you want, and to create the life you want. It is your birthright.

Following are some sample affirmations, ones that I have worked with personally. Let these serve as examples for you to create your own.

> *I have inner peace and contentment – true success!*
> *I have total freedom to do whatever I wish.*
> *I now create world peace and transformation.*
> *I am an open channel for exquisite, endlessly abundant creativity, in many, many forms.*
> *I have real personal confidence, and a very positive self-image.*
> *I am connected deeply, intimately, with my higher self, and my enlightenment.*

*I have beautiful, harmonious, satisfying rela-
    tionships.*
*I am in perfect health, for as long as I wish, in
    this body.*
*I have physical strength and attractiveness, for
    as long as I wish, in this body.*
My income exceeds my expenses.
*My connection with infinite intelligence is
    now easily yielding me a vast personal
    fortune.*

Work and play with one, two, or three at a time — as
many as you feel you can handle — until you achieve
results.

A common error

I must point out a common error many people
make when they begin doing affirmations: it is the error
of assuming the affirmations themselves will do all the
work, and that there is nothing else that needs to be
done.

In many cases, it is true that nothing else other than
the affirmation needs to be done to accomplish what is
intended. In these cases, all that is necessary is for us to
suggest the affirmation to our subconscious, and the
forces are set in motion which automatically create
what we desire. This is the power of our human energy
— our conscious and subconscious states of mind.
When you see this happen — as I have many times — it
is an exciting and fulfilling experience.

But there are many types of affirmations which
need to be supported by and completed through a very
mechanical series of actions in the world. Affirmations

for abundance or creative expression or finding the perfect job, for example, need to be done along with very logical steps in the world. These steps are simple to discover — you either know them already, or they may take some research.

In creating abundance, for example, you have to find the service or product you can offer the world, which you will be paid abundantly for. Then you have to list the steps necessary to make that service or product available: you may need to make a brochure, make samples, do an ad, etc.

I have known people who have affirmed abundance, and then found an unexpected check in the mail, or inherited money they hadn't known about. But most people who are successfully affirming abundance find that they have to do the necessary groundwork to offer their talents and abilities to the world.

Keep doing your affirmation, and it will become clear to you what you need to do.

Have patience

The other necessary element for you to create your own personal freedom in whatever ways you wish is patience and persistence. The world wasn't created in a day. Occasionally you'll find an affirmation which manifests almost as soon as you say it. But most created things take some time to manifest. Give a seed a week or so to sprout. Then give the plant a few weeks or even months to develop. Give an affirmation at least three weeks to create some results. In the case of an affirmation as broad as *"My connection with infinite intelligence is now easily yielding me a vast personal fortune,"* it may take years to fully manifest. But you should be able to feel changes and see results within three weeks after affirming it every day. In this example, you'll find yourself discovering creative ways to make money. You won't be nearly so broke, and you'll be *feeling* a lot more abundant — even if your bank account hasn't changed much in three weeks. It will grow, if you have patience and are persistent.

One affirmation which worked for me almost instantly was *"I am organized."* For years I had been telling myself that I was disorganized. But as soon as I affirmed to myself, just a few times in a single session, "I am organized," I felt the truth of that statement fill my being. I got up from my chair and immediately started listing all of the things I was planning to do, hoping to do, and dreaming of doing. Then I organized it all, putting it into a list with the first priorities at the top. In one moment, I ceased looking at myself as a limited, unorganized person, and saw myself as being very capable of clear organization. It was simple. Within a few weeks, I had created a filing system for both personal and business affairs, I had cleaned up my desk and personal work area, and had gotten into a daily habit of listing everything I intended to do, numbering it in priorities, and handling it.

If you are ready for it, some of your affirmations may manifest that quickly for you. But usually, it will take longer. But keep it up, every day (or at least three or four times a week). If one particular affirmation seems to lose its energy for you, if it feels lifeless, if you aren't connecting with it, find another way to say it that feels good and strong to you.

If you find no noticeable results in three weeks, try writing your affirmations and your resistances. Discover which of these resistances are blocking you from creating your good. Then find affirmations which are the opposite.

It is a startling thing for many people to realize that *we create what we want*. We may not be creating what we think we want, but in fact we are creating that which we want on some deep, perhaps subconscious, levels. If you're broke, it's because you want to be, or because you feel you deserve to be, or because you feel you can't handle money. Find some affirmations which change your thinking about these things. If you're alone, it's because you want to be. There's no other excuse. If you really feel you don't want to be alone, and are ready for an ideal relationship, affirm it to yourself, and you'll create it for yourself. All it takes is a strong, focused affirmation with feeling behind it, and patience, and persistence.

The law of karma

Affirmations work only for the good — that is, the highest good of all concerned. If anyone wishes to use these tools for their own 'good' at the expense of another, they will create problems for themselves. This is because they are neglecting the law of *karma*. Briefly stated, the law of karma says that the Universe is set up so that whatever you do comes back to you. Think loving thoughts and you live in a loving world. Think hateful thoughts and you live in a hate-filled world. Try to injure someone else, and you will be injured.

This is why there is never any reason to fear misuse of these powerful tools — or to fear black magic or witches (in the negative sense of the word) or even the effects of chemicals or atomic energy — because any people who try to harm others, through affirmations or ignorance or any other means, only end up hurting themselves. The law of karma is infallible. If you have even the slightest feeling that what you're affirming may not be the best thing for you, or for someone else, finish your affirming with the words, *"This, or something better, is now manifesting for the highest good of all concerned."*

Then just sit back and relax and enjoy the fruits of your creation. Let it come to you, easily and effortlessly, without struggling, striving, or suffering.

Easily and effortlessly

I'll close this chapter with mention of a particularly power affirmation for people in the world today:

> *"_____ comes to me, easily and effortlessly."*

Fill in the blank with whatever you desire.

Often, one of the largest stumbling blocks in the way of attaining or accomplishing something, especially our most cherished dreams and goals, is that we're trying too hard.

Life does not have to be a struggle. Look at the trees and plants and birds and other animals. Are they struggling for survival? "Consider the lilies of the field . . . ."

Simply affirm to yourself,

> *"Freedom comes to me, easily and effortlessly."*
> *"Love . . .*
> *"Money . . .*

"Abundance...
"Happiness...

And also specific things, such as,

"My perfect artistic expression comes to me,
easily and effortlessly."
"My book...
"My creative expression...

Even very specific projects and commitments can be finished and fulfilled, easily and effortlessly, with this affirmation.

When you ask the Universe for something, you will receive it — unless you're denying it on deeper levels of your being. Let it all come to you, easily and effortlessly. You deserve it. You deserve to have it all. And now you are holding in your own hands the tools to create whatever you want... whatever your heart desires.

Remember, you chose your relationships — whether consciously or unconsciously. . . . They are happening for your evolution — for your growth into true freedom and creativity and happiness.

IV

Relationships

Our relationships with others — both casual and intimate — give us a constant, truthful mirror of ourselves. If you have created generally loving, supportive relationships in your life, give yourself some appreciation — you obviously are being loving and supportive yourself. If you have created difficult relationships, with anger and resentment involved, look into yourself to find the source of your anger and resentment. That other person isn't 'doing it to you' or 'making you angry' — you are doing it to yourself, you are making yourself angry. That other person is doing you a favor, by providing you with someone who makes you aware of your areas of unconsciousness, and points out where you need to change in order to be truly free. We should thank those that we have difficult relationships with, rather than blame them: They are our best teachers.

An honest appraisal of our relationships can provide us with some of the best material we have to help us grow. Within the experiences of our relationships are keys to freedom. Let's find these keys, because they're within us all.

Tantric relationships

Every relationship we have is a *tantric* relationship, if we see it in that light. That is, every relationship is a deep sharing which we have created in order to learn and grow, every moment. We may not have been conscious of this fact, but there are deep reasons for all of our relationships, both intimate and otherwise.

Look at every deep, ongoing relationship which you've had. Unless you've been closed off to it, you can see how much you've learned in the sharing you've had together. You've each had things to teach each other, and that is why you were drawn together. You've mirrored each other, in many ways. You've reflected each other's strength and beauty and positive qualities, and you've shown each other where you each need to change and grow. And you each have grown, whether you've wanted to or not. You've each taken on some of the characteristics of the other person.

Sometimes this has been for the good: you've become a clearer, more experienced person in the process. And sometimes this has been a negative influence, if the people you've chosen to share your time with have had qualities which didn't serve them or you to become better people. Either way, you change and, eventually, grow. Either way, it's a tantric relationship.

What do you want?

It's important to realize that, in our relationships as

in most other areas of our lives, *we're free to create whatever we desire.* We have evolved enough, as a people and as individuals, to go beyond the need for a single social morality which is dictated to all, and enforced, like the law of Moses. Morality can be a purely individual choice, and it is up to each of us to decide in our hearts and minds which is right for us, and to live by that, as long as we don't use it to harm others. We can have any kind of relationship(s) we want. This is certainly the meaning of true personal freedom.

Most of what follows focuses on intimate, personal relationships. But the same principles apply to all relationships: friend, parent-child, boss-employee, co-worker, neighbor, etc. Many people who are unhappy and lonely, in fact, have more success in creating the kind of perfect relationships they want if they first start with getting more satisfaction from the friend and co-worker and other relationships they already have, and then go on to focusing on and creating an intimate romantic relationship after they have a little practice in being a good friend.·

Sondra Ray, author of *I Deserve Love,* uses a process in her workshops that is very startling and eye-opening for a lot of people:

> *Make the following lists across the top of a sheet of paper:*
>
> What I want   What I have   What I really want
>
> *Under "What I want," list what you want — in your relationships, in your life in general. Under "What I have," list what you have at present. Then, under "What I really want,"*

also list what you have at present — *because*
we have already created in our lives what we
have really wanted.

Some people may feel this isn't true, because it
often certainly doesn't seem to be true on conscious
levels of our awareness. We don't consciously think that
we want to be alone, or in very unsupportive or unhappy
relationships, or in poverty, or whatever. But on deeper
levels, it is completely true: we have created for ourselves exactly what we have wanted and what we have
felt we deserved; we have created for ourselves at present what we feel we are worthy of. But we deserve
better things — so let's start creating some better
things!

First, we need to focus on the inner planes — purely
within ourselves, within our beliefs and imaginations.
Once we do some inner investigation and work, we'll
focus on the outer plane, which involves our actions in
the world, with our partner or partners, and with
everyone else we relate to.

The inner planes

As we have seen in the previous chapter, all creation begins as a subtle, spiritual impulse, then becomes
a thought, then a feeling, and then it is manifested on
the outer, material plane.

What we have created so far in relationship is a
result of what we have been affirming to ourselves over
the years. It is a result of what we have been thinking
and feeling and believing. Through conscious effort, we
can let go of thoughts and beliefs which are creating
what we don't want, and replace them instead with

thoughts and beliefs which create what we do want.

Let go of the belief that you are in any way incapable of satisfying relationships! It is not a true belief — we are all capable of satisfying relationships. Quit telling yourself that you don't deserve a satisfying relationship, or that you're selfish or unloving in your relationships. The truth is you do deserve a wonderful relationship, and that you are basically loving and giving. Refuse to believe any longer that you can't have what you want, because you can, if you believe you can. Let go of all those unsupportive and negative thoughts and beliefs, and replace them with some supportive and positive ones, and you will start seeing some very satisfying results, almost instantly.

The best way to overcome any and all negative conditioning we have given ourselves or accepted from others in terms of relationships is through mental imagery and affirmations. When negative thoughts arise, counter with positive ones. Create a picture of yourself as being able to create ideal relationships, even if you have to suspend your beliefs otherwise. What have you got to lose?

It is very important — essential, in fact — for us to create a clear picture or idea of what we want in relationship, and to affirm that it is so. Look honestly at what you truly want. Imagine it clearly in your mind's eye. We must first create in our thoughts and feelings those things we wish to create in our lives.

Allow yourself delicious fantasies. Picture your perfect lover: Imagine your first meeting; imagine that you are confident and poised; imagine a beautiful, loving relationship blossoming. Then affirm, *"This, or something better, is now manifesting for the highest good of all concerned."*

If you are currently involved in a relationship which you want to continue, imagine it expanding and changing to become your ideal. Imagine the best possible relationship for all concerned.

A great master once said, *"Ask and it shall be given to you."* It's unfortunate that there are so many who deny that this is true, because they end up creating that which they believe, a life of unhappiness and a lack of fulfillment of their real potential. But if we believe it, if we ask for it, if we see that we truly deserve it, we will create whatever we want in our lives. Try it and see for yourself.

When I came to the point where I decided, after many years of open relationships, that I wanted to find one person to focus on, and to build a committed relationship with, I simply said, forcefully, to myself, "All right, Universe, I'm ready to fall in love and be completely immersed in a wonderful, exciting relationship!" I said it just two or three times, with emotion. Just two days later, I met her, and I knew within an hour that she was the one the Universe was giving me — she was the one I asked for.

The importance of our work on the inner planes in creating anything is in some ways contradictory to what most of us were educated to believe. We too often tend to deal with things on a level which is habitually *outer*-directed. We think that the thing we need to do in order to create a relationship we want is to go out and meet somebody somewhere. But if we awaken to the understanding that the most important work is on the *inner* planes — within our hearts and minds and emotions — we will be much more successful in creating whatever we desire. We simply need to connect, each in our own way, with our abilities to creatively imagine what we wish. You deserve relationships which are loving and supportive. Begin creating them right now with a daily affirmation session.

Some particularly powerful affirmations for creating relationships are:

> *"I deserve love!"*
> *"I feel good about having what I want in relationship."*
> *"I now have a wonderful sex life."*
> *"I now have a beautiful, harmonious, satisfying relationship."*

Make up your own affirmations. And don't ever invalidate their power... "ask and you shall receive."

The outer plane

As soon as you are ready for relationship, it happens. Then it becomes something to skillfully manage on the outer plane as well as the inner.

The key to successful relationships on the outer level can be given in one word: *communication*. Communication simply involves sharing your feelings — giving other people your honest feedback, both positive and negative, and receiving feedback in a way which is beneficial. But so many people have not discovered how to take feedback so that it works for them! A very perceptive counselor and teacher named Shirley Luthman explains that there are four possible reactions to feedback, which we all have experienced, especially if the other person's communication involves something which confronts us with something which is hard for us to accept. The four reactions are:

(1) *Denial.* We simply refuse to accept what others are telling us. We tell them it isn't true, that they don't understand, etc.

(2) *Defense.* We create all kinds of excuses. We explain why it is that things have worked out in such a way that prevent us from taking responsibility for our actions.

(3) *Beating ourselves up.* We admit that they're right in their observation, and then we use that to create guilt, fear, worry, and other negative self-images for ourselves.

(4) *Simply accepting it and letting it sink in.* This is the only responsible, effective reaction to another's communication. We simply hear what they're saying, we realize that there's some reason for them to be telling us those particular things, and we accept what they're saying and agree to look at it. If, after a while, we feel they're being accurate, we acknowledge that, thank them, and see if there's some way to improve things. If on the other hand we feel, after some quiet introspection, that their communication was not useful, we simply let it go, without blaming or judging anyone in the process.

As an example, I'll tell you something which happened to me recently. I was sitting around with several close friends, who had known me for years. I made a comment about wanting a cup of coffee, and one of my friends said she thought I drank entirely too much coffee. Some of the others agreed. My reactions to their communication went through all four of the possibilities above, in order:

First, I simply denied it: I simply said it wasn't true. I didn't drink too much coffee. I am strong and healthy and my body enjoys it, so there's nothing wrong with it, nothing excessive about it.

Then, I started defending myself. I said I loved coffee, and it's part of my heritage because my family drinks so much of it. I love the ritual of it, and the closeness of people drinking it together. I love the stimulation of it — it's good for writing and other creative things. And I asked them why they were so uptight about it, and accused them of being puritanical about what they eat and drink.

They continued to be adamant, not believing my defense. So I eventually started to agree with them, but then soon began to feel guilty for doing things which were self-destructive. Maybe I am a hopeless addict . . . maybe I am a weak person . . . .

I soon realized that these doubts and feelings of guilt were useless, as are all self-doubts and guilt feelings. I saw that my friends were giving me some good information, based on clear perceptions of me. They certainly weren't trying to make me feel guilty or worthless — they were simply pointing out an area of my life that they felt I could improve. I then found it very easy to just accept what they were saying, without denying, defending, or beating myself up. I just absorbed their communication, and after a while decided to cut way down on the amount of coffee I drink. I found it very easy to go from six or eight cups a day to just one or two. And I've felt better physically as a result, too. I later thanked my friends for their honest feedback. It is something I value more than anything else in the world.

Our friends, lovers, bosses, parents, children, and everyone else we encounter often mirror us, and give us valuable instructions which can help us uplevel the quality of our lives if we're open to their communications — if we learn to listen, and stop denying, defending, and beating ourselves up with what they're telling us.

Negotiation

Another essential key to successful, supportive relationships is contained in a word which some people have difficulty relating to: *negotiation*. True negotiation is *the art of creating win-win situations.* If either person in the relationship is not winning, that is, not getting what they want and deserve, then the relationship is not working.

So many people plunge into intimate, long-lasting relationships without ever taking the time to sit down with the other person involved and clearly spell out what they want in the relationship! The result is that a huge amount of time and energy is often spent over the following months and years trying to get what they want out of the relationship while creating frustration and resentment instead.

Often this frustration can be dissolved with a few simple conversations in which each person communicates as clearly as they can exactly what they want in the relationship. Then the other person responds, saying from their heart what they feel good about giving. It is often necessary to work out a compromise, but it is far better to compromise than to spend years trying to get something that your partner doesn't feel good about giving.

Keep focusing on the fact that it is always possible to come up with a creative solution which will give you both what you want. It may be something you've never done before, but there *is* a creative solution. Or, one or both of you may choose to end the relationship — that too is a possibility. Separation is sometimes a much better choice than years of frustration. You might have to create another relationship in which you're in greater alignment with your partner.

Dealing with conflict

Here is a very good thing to do if and when you find yourself locked into a conflict with your partner — if you're fighting or struggling, or if you're stuck in certain positions that don't seem flexible enough to work together:

(1) Stop. *Take a breath.* Don't wait for your partner to do it — it takes two to tangle, but it takes only one to stop.

(2) Give your partner the time, space, and encouragement to totally express their feelings. *Listen* to them . . . don't interrupt them (you'll get your turn) . . . don't even judge them, especially if they're upset. Just give them the opportunity to express themselves, completely. This works wonders to 'blow off charges' that may have been deeply buried for a long time. Remember, don't interrupt! Sometimes it may seem very difficult not to interrupt to defend yourself or to invalidate their point of view, or whatever. But don't interrupt. Just open up to it and listen to it all. Encourage them to say what is on their mind, even if it makes you furious. Wait until they have had their say, and tell them, "Thank you for sharing that with me."

(3) Now it's your turn to *express your feelings*. Be sure that it is clear with your partner that you want them to give you the space to let out all of your feelings just as you have let them do. Tell them they must not interrupt but just listen to what you have to say. They'll

get their chance to respond. Then tell them all of your feelings, all the things you've been telling yourself that you didn't dare tell them before: tell them why you're upset, or angry, or whatever. Put it out there, even if it sounds stupid or selfish or unflattering. Let yourself say anything and everything about your partner and the situation you've created together. Don't try to edit or censor or soften it — jump into the center of the poison, and show your partner your deepest feelings.

The next step depends on how effective the last two have been. If you've both said it all, you'll notice that the charge between you has dissipated, because you've released a lot of the 'stuff' you were holding onto. But if one or both of you still feels agitated, repeat steps (2) and (3) again, each of you taking another turn to express your feelings. Perhaps something your partner said really made you furious, or depressed, or whatever. Share whatever feelings arise. These steps have been effective when you begin to feel calmer and closer than you were when you began.

(4) Next, ask your partner *what they want from you*. Give them the time, space, and encouragement to tell you exactly what they want and need from you. Listen and remember.

(5) Then, tell your partner exactly *what you want from them*. Be open and honest. Spell out what you want and need. One way to get into it, if you have difficulty doing it, is to play a little game with each other, in which each of you spells out your 'ideal scene': if you could have the relationship exactly as you would want it in its most ideal form, what would it be? This will show you what you truly want in the relationship. Now comes the final step: the *negotiation*. Don't shy away from the word 'negotiation' because it sounds too

cold or too businesslike. Negotiation is really the essential basis of every relationship: we are together because we have some reason for being together, and that reason involves giving something and receiving something from the other person. If the relationship isn't working smoothly, it is because the agreements haven't been spelled out clearly enough. (You can call it 'making agreements' if negotiation is not the right word for you.)

Negotiate with your partner. Make clear agreements. Find out what your partner wants from you, and clearly express what you feel good about giving them. Ask for what you want, and find some area of agreement with your partner. Each of you must do what feels good to you. You may have to compromise, but never allow one person to violate the other.

If this exercise does not work for you, if repeating these steps does not clear the air and resolve your feelings, you may need to seek a counselor or a skilled facilitator to assist you in learning to share your feelings in an effective way. Our deepest tantric relationships tend to bring out our deepest feelings and emotional patterns, and many of us need some help in learning to explore and express our feelings in a way which doesn't create more negativity. All too often, we tend to 'dump' negative feelings on our partners, criticizing or blaming them, rather than staying with our own deepest feelings and expressing them in a way which is honest and even vulnerable, and doesn't deny the other person's feelings.

Enlightened relationships are just like enlightened business: they are a win-win proposition. Everybody wins, nobody loses. Your partner has told you what they want from you. Now you tell them what you feel good about giving them. Tell them what things you can do for them, and what things you cannot do. Be honest and don't violate your own feelings.

Be creative — there are no set norms or forms that you have to follow. A great change is taking place in the mass consciousness, a change which allows each person to live their lives as they wish. You can have any type of relationship(s) you want!

Every relationship has the potential to become the perfect relationship, if and when the inner and outer levels are harmoniously in balance. Keep remembering both the inner and outer levels of activity in your relationships. Keep remembering that there is always the option to go within yourself, and to affirm that which you truly wish to create, or to open yourself, completely, to the other(s) in the relationship, and fully express your feelings, and tell them what you want, and arrange to get what you want, and to give the others what they want.

Some people find the inner plane more easy to deal with, and some find they are more skillful on the outer plane. The key is to learn to deal with them both, in perfect balance. They support each other: the more you learn about one way of being, the more you learn about the other.

Jealousy, fear and anger

Jealousy is a common experience for so many people in relationship. It is a deep, subtle and sometimes even violent conglomeration of emotions — mostly fear and anger. Like all emotions, it is something to be respected, and something to be examined.

I used to believe that it was possible to reach a state where jealousy is fully transcended. There are some teachers today who claim it is possible, and they may be right. I have found in my own life that, when I tried to have open relationships, there were times when my 'primary' lover had other sexual encounters and I felt no jealousy at all. But there were times when I was very jealous. And there were other times when I found myself feeling that I was accepting the situation in general, but there were a lot of little specific things I was irritated and critical with — in other words, I was still very jealous.

As I look back today, I find myself wondering whether I transcended my feelings of jealousy *at all* — or whether I had just repressed those feelings because I didn't want to confront them. I'm beginning to feel that jealousy is something to simply accept rather than something to even try to transcend — at least at this stage of my growth.

The most important step in creating any kind of true, deep freedom within a relationship is to totally accept the feelings of jealousy you may sometimes have, and your lover (or lovers) may sometimes have. It's okay to be you, it's okay for others to be themselves, it's okay to be jealous, and angry, and fearful.

Accept your feelings, completely. This is the first step toward rising above them and transmuting them into the highest creative energies. When we accept our feelings, we are no longer giving them the power of our resistance. What we resist tends to stay with us. Once we let resistance go, we can truly let everything go which we don't want to hold on to. This is a key to freedom.

Jealousy, anger, fear must first be accepted; then, as we teach ourselves how to let them go, they will soon dissolve. This can become our focus: to accept the jealousy, fear, and anger in ourselves and in others completely, and then to find the skillful means to overcome these separating feelings.

Our focus becomes a matter of finding *skillful means* — means which are different in each different situation, and for each different person. 'Skillful means' are endless, just as the path of our evolution is endless.

Keep this in mind in your relationships with all others: You can create whatever kinds of relationships your heart desires. You can have totally open, free, loving relationships with as many or as few people as you want. Just remember to keep as open as possible to everyone involved. Or you may decide to remain completely monogamous in order to minimize feelings of jealousy, and focus deeply on one intimate relationship. This is certainly a choice which is appropriate for a great many people.

Remember, it is your small self, your limited self, that is behind any separation you feel from anyone. And it is your higher self that is moving into openness, friendliness, oneness with others.

Don't reject your feelings of separation and jealousy and anger and fear. Just accept them, and let them pass. You don't need them at all. Affirm to yourself:

I am open, to all people at all times . . . .
Like the Sun, I shine my light on everyone . . . .
I am an open vessel, filled with divine love . . . .

Sharings

Just recently, while sitting down and having a drink and a talk with my lover, I realized that I have often been somewhat uncomfortable with the word 'relationship', even though I use it quite often. There's something about the word that is too serious, too heavy. It's not the meaning of the word itself, but it's the connotations that have piled up around the word over the years.

We both searched for a word that would say the same thing, but without the negative connotations. And we came up with the word *sharing*. Every relationship is certainly a sharing — a sharing of energy through time together — and the word sharing has such beautiful overtones.

Since that conversation, we now talk about our sharing more often than we talk about our relationship. And it feels very good to do so.

A key to fulfilling relationships

Give your lovers the freedom to be themselves, and find the freedom in your heart to be yourself. Trust and support the other person's power, and trust and support your own power. They are not in conflict. There is always a way to harmonize your feelings with your lover's feelings.

Trust and support the other person's experiences, insights, impulses, dreams, sharings. Support each other, and encourage each other to do what feels best in your hearts. It may mean spending time alone ... or with others ... or growing apart at times. Let it be.

Give your sharing a huge space in which to move, and grow, a space large enough for both of you, all of you, to be completely fulfilled.

There are an infinite number of approaches to solving any problem that comes up in relationship. Be creative —trust your own experience, your own feelings, for these give you the answers you are looking for, the ways to work it out.

You chose your relationships, your sharings — whether consciously or unconsciously. They are happening, and they are happening for a very good reason, whether you know it or not. They are happening for your evolution, for your growth into true freedom and creativity and happiness.

> *Love is the answer*
> *Love is the key*
> *It can open any door*
> *Give us eyes to see*
> *In our hearts lies a secret*
> *And it sets us free:*
> *All we need is love . . .*
> *All we need is love!*

*It is time we saw sex as being the
truly sacred act that it is:
a deep meditation . . .
a dance of the forces of creation.*

V

Sex

I would like to extend a warm welcome to all of you who are beginning to read this book at this particular chapter. I'd probably do the same thing. Sex is a vital force, a force to be understood, and dealt with — and so many people have not dealt with it effectively in our culture! They run from it, or feel trapped in it or frustrated with, or they keep searching for it — and find no satisfaction in any of these choices.

An important premise of this book is that we can find personal freedom by truly plunging into every feeling and desire of every moment — rejecting nothing, as long as we don't hurt anyone else. This is the teaching of tantra. It is more than the 'yoga of sex', as it is so often defined — it is the 'yoga of everything'. And that certainly includes sex, for most people in our culture.

Some questions for you to answer

Take a clear, honest look at your attitudes toward sex. Do you like it? Do you want it? Are parts of it shameful or immoral? Should you have it only with one person? Are you basically monogamous? Polygamous? Are you satisfied with your present sexual situation? Could it be improved? Do you have any views or feelings about sex which are limiting your personal freedom?

It doesn't matter how you answer these questions. You are a free being — your true nature is already absolutely free. So you can feel any way you want about sex, or relationships, or marriage, or anything and everything. But if you find that your views and beliefs are limiting your personal freedom, or keeping you from getting what you want in life, it's very useful to take a good, clear look at those beliefs. Plunge into them, examine them, and describe them clearly to yourself.

Whatever your sex life is, you might as well feel good about it! You're creating it for yourself, so you must have a good reason to do so. You may or may not be conscious of this, of course. But you can become conscious of it right now — if you just think about it for a moment. . . .

How do you feel about sex? How have you felt about your sexual relationships? Answer these questions honestly to yourself — the most important first step is just to be totally honest. Do you feel guilty about anything? Take some time to examine that one — guilt is a very popular state of mind in our culture today, unfortunately.

Look at this feeling and belief, for example: "I feel guilty when I have sex." Whether you are a man or a woman, you could be carrying that guilt around with you. Once you see it, once you are aware of it, you can do whatever you want with it. You can continue to feel that way, and either deny yourself sexual activity — which may be an appropriate alternative for some people — or you can continue your sexual activity and be run by your guilt into feeling limited and resentful. Or you can see that those guilt feelings are no longer serving you, and you can let them go. You can affirm that *exactly the opposite* is true. You can say to yourself, repeatedly and with emotion, "It's okay to have sex when I want to," or, "I feel good about my sex life." And your experience of feeling guilt will start to change, to weaken. You can then take it a step further — if these words feel right to you (if not, make up your own!) — and affirm, "Having sex is fun and satisfying," or, "I feel wonderful when I have sex," or even, "Having sex frees me!"

Sondra Ray has produced a cassette of affirmations on which she affirms a great number of things which help people loosen up their sexual attitudes, including, "My parents feel good about my sex life," and even, "My minister feels good about my sex life!" As long as you're going to continue to do it, you might as well let go of the guilt you've developed which surrounds it.

A recent *Readers' Digest* article presented an extensive amount of research which confirmed that there is a great schism in America today between what people think is right and moral about sexual behavior, and what people actually do sexually. This is especially true of a great many men, who want their wives or lovers to be 'faithful' to them, and who feel that they should be 'faithful', and yet feel a need to 'indulge' in outside sex. This is the classic double-standard, and it is damaging to the relationships involved and damaging to the people who practice it — unless there is a clear agree-

ment which feels good to everyone involved. What can
be done about this? The only lasting answer can be
found in total honesty, negotiation, and trust.

Trust yourself!

Trust and respect your own impulses and your own
personal power. Trust that this will lead you to discovering the lifestyle which is appropriate for you.

So many people are afraid to act on their own feelings, and they are trapping themselves by not doing so.
Don't be afraid of your feelings, even if they seem extreme. Within your feelings are important lessons for
you to learn. Within your feelings are the keys to your
personal freedom.

When I started to realize that I was actually creating my life exactly as I wanted it, a lot of changes
happened in my life. Sexually, I became more and more
open. I saw that I had often dreamed of a great deal of
openness, and suddenly I was free to try anything. In my
fantasies, I wanted to try group sex, and I wanted to try
massage parlors, and prostitutes. These were things
which were forbidden, and tantalizing just because they
were forbidden — like bars were before I turned 21. So I
gave myself permission to do all of these things. I
plunged into my fantasies and lived them out. The experiences were invaluable.

I found that group sex was not at all satisfying. I
found it to be disconcerting and unfulfilling, because I
couldn't focus on one person, and I couldn't satisfy two
people at once. Sex with one other person, I came to
realize, is much more fulfilling, because you can give
that person your total attention and total being.

I tried massage parlors, and prostitutes on the

streets, too. The experiences themselves were somewhat enjoyable at first, but later felt shallow and painful. I found that the women didn't want to relate to me as a person — they just wanted to get their money, get on with it, get it over with, and get on to their next 'trick'. I couldn't blame them, but I lost interest in the whole scene very quickly.

And, even more importantly, I found that I felt very bad afterwards. I felt as if I had done something which had violated those women, and violated myself. I felt that I had done something which was not in alignment with my purpose for being on this planet. And so, by letting myself do the most extreme things I could imagine sexually, I saw them for what they were for me — unfulfilling and shallow. And so those experiences were very valuable for me. If I had not allowed myself the freedom to experience those fantasies, I would still be carrying those desires around with me — deeply buried, for the most part, but there nevertheless.

Do what you have the energy to do. If you follow your feelings, you'll never go wrong. You may do something extreme, like I did. But you'll find a much greater clarity about yourself afterwards, if you examine your own feelings about what you've done.

It's all right to do something extreme once in a while. I have a rule of thumb about this:

> *Everything in moderation... and that includes some excess (in moderation)...*

I've known too many people who have become excessively moderate, and have become afraid of their deepest feelings and impulses — afraid, basically, of themselves, and stuck in rigid models of what they should and should not do. That kind of moderation is not a very effective way to become truly free.

Sexual energy

There is a beautiful, dynamic source of energy in the universe, waiting to be tapped — the energy between a man and a woman, the energy of creation. (If you're gay, you could substitute "the energy between two women" or "the energy between two men." Tantra embraces everything, rejecting nothing — so of course it embraces gay lifestyles too. Don't be put off by the male-female orientation of this book. Substitute your own changes where necessary.)

Much has been written and taught about *transmuting* sexual energy. But, in my experience, this is unnecessary and redundant, for sexual energy transmutes itself. If our sexual energy is allowed to move through our bodies — if we aren't blocking it through guilt or other limiting beliefs — we experience a physical, emotional, mental, and spiritual transmutation of energy. This can happen whether we're making love, meditating, or masturbating.

How does this take place? Our body is an energy system. Different parts of our bodies are different centers of energy. Our sexual organs contain a very powerful source of energy. By focusing on this energy, physically arousing it or just mentally concentrating upon it, we find that it is a *dynamic* force — it moves. If we let it move as it will, we find that its natural movement is upward, through our abdomen, into our hearts, and still upward through the so-called 'higher' centers of energy and glandular activity located in the throat, the forehead, and the top of the skull. This energy can then literally shower over our entire being, rejuvenating, purifying, healing, strengthening. Making love opens our hearts, and opens our minds.

So many people, by trying to be either moral or spiritual, are cutting themselves off from their own sources of power in their so-called 'lower' centers of energy! Many people on 'spiritual' paths have beliefs very similar to those which were popular in Europe in Shakespeare's time; some teachers from India teach that sexual orgasm weakens the system, and that the energy needs to be held in and drawn up into the higher centers to awaken true freedom and enlightenment. The result — except possibly for a very few people who may not be suited for sexual expression — is a massive amount of repression, self-denial, and guilt. I know, because I've tried that path. And I've known many others who have tried — and many who are still trying. I found that celibacy doesn't work for most Americans, myself included. It requires too much a denial of our feelings, desires, and impulses. It leads to a rejection of ourselves and our culture, creating more problems than it solves. It is not an effective path to freedom, for most Americans.

I don't mean to deny the value of celibacy for the people who are involved in it and who feel they are getting something worthwhile from it. Many priests, for example, may desire sexual experience, but feel that their level of dedication, service, and personal example would deteriorate if they 'indulged' sexually. The path of tantra embraces all paths — even those who deny or withhold their sexual energy. The path of tantra teaches me to accept everyone and every other path, even those who criticize or condemn me for saying what I have to say. Every person must find their own way, in their hearts.

In my experience, sexual energy is not something to be denied in any way. It is something to be celebrated, to be enjoyed, and to be used as a vehicle for complete personal freedom. This is the path of tantra — the way which feels right in my heart, and which seems most appropriate for the Western culture in general. Our bodies are miraculous creations — things to be respected, admired, appreciated, enjoyed. A deep truth which emerges from metaphysical and spiritual study is that we are all God-like beings; we all create our own experience — we even create our own bodies, through our deepest mental imagery and affirmations. So when a man admires a woman walking down the street, it is God admiring his own creation. And that woman herself is God enjoying her own creation.

Sex is more than a natural impulse — it is a deeply sacred act, whether it is part of our deepest relationships, or even whether it is a very casual, impulsive thing with a person we may hardly know.

Joining our bodies creates a special 'temple', through the force of two spirits, two energy fields, two auras, blending totally into one. A magnetic energy flows between the two bodies, which is deeply healing, strengthening, refreshing. It is a profound opening . . . a letting go . . . a perfect, wordless meditation upon the creative forces of life.

Tantric sex

Ancient tantric sex practices are described, sometimes literally, sometimes symbolically, in many books. There are two exquisite tantric temples which still stand in India, adorned with thousands of statues of different sexual positions and practices (although today, unfortunately, the Indian guides to these temples seem oblivious to them, even embarrassed by them, trying to make people believe that they are somehow metaphorical rather than physical — when they are obviously explicit and extremely un-Victorian). Many of the ancient tantric practices involve elaborate preparations, which often celebrate all of the senses — including different foods (including meat and fish and wine) for taste, flowers for sight, incense for smell, bells and other musical instruments for sound, and our bodies for touch.

The most important element in the sexual practices is the acceptance and enjoyment of all of the things which give us pleasure and an appreciation of beauty. There is nothing to reject in our sexual energy and our sexual relationships — there is beauty and wonder in each eternal moment of our lives.

Make up your own tantric practices — these are the most appropriate practices for you. You are free to do whatever you wish. You are free to live out your deepest, most soaring, most outrageous fantasies.

One beautiful way to make love

The following is a specific practice which I particularly love. Let it serve as a model for you to create your own — for the rituals you devise will be perfectly suited to you. Take your time for this kind of love-making.

Lie with your partner... or sit together....
Bask in the beautiful simplicity of just being with each other, silently, quietly.

See, and enjoy, and caress each other's bodies....

At some time, the man says to the woman, focusing on her body, 'This is the temple'.

At some time, the woman says to the man, focusing on his body, 'This is the temple'.

At some time, the woman focuses on the man's beautiful sexual organs, his creative erection, and says, 'This is the key to the temple'....

At some time, the man focuses on the woman's beautiful sexual organs, the center of the depths of her being, and says, 'This is the entrance to the temple'....

Then the key is slowly and gently placed into the entrance... and each says, in their own way, in their own time, 'We are in the temple.... We are receiving the blessings of the Universe'... (or you can say the 'blessings of God', or whatever you feel like saying from your heart, from the depths of your being).

Then feel, as totally, as sensitively as you can, the energy of the Universe flowing through you, blessing you, giving you eternal youth, eternal vitality. Feel how good it is to be alive... feel your natural divinity... your connection with the source of existence.

It is time we saw sex as the truly sacred act which it is: a deep meditation... a dance of the forces of creation.

Sustaining sexual energy

Some men — especially young men — sometimes find it difficult to sustain their sexual energy long enough to give their partners a truly deep and fulfilling experience. Stimulation is so intense for men that they sometimes find it difficult to control. There are a few simple techniques which can prevent this, and give the man as much control when making love as he wishes, allowing him to reach a climax just as his partner does.

One technique is mental. The others are physical.

(1) In your mind's eye, circulate the energy through your body when making love. The intense stimulation is centered purely on your sexual organs, so move the energy up your spine, and circulate it around your body and your partner's body. This will allow you to make love for a much longer period of time.

(2) When in deep penetration with your partner, the man should move more in a circular pattern than in a straight in-and-out pattern if he wants to make it last longer. This is much more exciting for the woman, and relatively less exciting for the man, giving the woman plenty of time to catch up with the man's level of excitement.

(3) Try using a condom. Natural skin condoms still give the man a great deal of sensitivity, but they are somewhat less stimulating.

(4) The final technique is part of the "chaotic meditation" taught by Bhagwan Rajneesh, a well-known teacher and prolific author from India. Shortly after doing this exercise, I discovered that it strengthened me sexually in a new way, giving me as much control and time to prolong and enjoy as I wanted. Do it when you're alone. It may seem peculiar or ir-

relevant — but give it a try. I don't, however, recommend it to anyone with a heart condition, because it is
very strenuous.

>*Put your hands up over your head, and
>jump up and down vigorously for ten (10!)
>minutes while shouting "Hu!" with force,
>breathing from your diaphragm (i.e., deeply,
>down in your stomach, and lower) every time
>you land on your feet. After two minutes,
>you'll probably be exhausted. But go beyond
>your imaginary physical limits, and you'll find
>that you can jump for ten minutes quite easily,
>once you get into it. Don't strain, but do jump
>energetically. Then relax.*

Afterward, you'll find that your muscles in your
abdominal area are much stronger, and that you have a
source of power and energy within you that is much
more potent than anything you've ever imagined.

To come or not to come?

Some teachers of "tantra" define tantric sex as sex
in which you don't reach an orgasm, but meditate
deeply together for a long period. This is a beautiful way
to make love — but certainly not the only way to make
love. In my opinion, tantric sex includes all kinds of sex,
rejecting nothing. Come if you wish, or don't come —
whatever your heart desires.

Making love

Following is a very special poem — one which

perhaps says more than a thousand pages of other words.

I didn't write it — it was given to me, channeled through me, during that exquisite period of meditation we call making love. I have printed it elsewhere — but it bears reprinting here, for it is worth reading again.

One golden, sunlit morning, I began to make love with my lover in a large bed with windows on two sides, with sunlight streaming in through the trees. I felt the energy rise as we got more deeply involved; soon it seemed to be connecting us with the sunlight, connecting us with the source of creation. It was an ecstatic experience.

At that moment, I heard a voice, almost shouting — euphorically — in my mind . . . and I realized it was a strange sort of poem. I tried to ignore it, but couldn't — it demanded to be written down. So I had to excuse myself for a moment, find a pen and paper, and write the first verse. Then we went back to our love-making. Then I heard a second verse. My writing and our love-making continued for a long time — maybe two hours, maybe longer, I have no idea of the time. And when we were through, the poem was finished.

It says a great deal about the deep truths of tantra. It is titled, appropriately enough,

Making Love

> *I remember every lover*
> *With such sweet feelings*
> *I dream of divine dakinis*
> *With such sweet prayer*
> *Every woman is a blessing —*
> *God's creation*
> *Every body is a miracle —*
> *The mind's revelation*

Every moment of love —
  Sweet inspiration!
Every one is Divine
  As they open to their depths
Such exquisite ritual
  Sweet meditation!
The forces of creation
  Unfolding within us
The Kingdom of Heaven
  Is truly within us

Remember the myths
  From our deep past heritage —
Leda and the Swan . . .
  Europa and the Bull . . .
The form of God appearing
  In a shower of gold
To a woman of exquisite
  Divine earthly beauty!

In love are all the teachings —
  The deep truths of tantra —
In love are all the forces
  Of the Universe on display
For all to see, to catch,
  To understand
And to enjoy the Bliss
  Of Union of the Divine

Within every woman —
  The forces of the Moon
Within every man —
  The forces of the Sun
Moon unites with the Sun

Eclipsing into One
And a New Moon is born,
And we are reborn,
Continuously reborn!

Within every woman —
The forces of the Earth
Within every man —
The forces of the Skies
Earth and Sky unite
And Heaven is here!
Totally illumined,
If we but understand it
Totally blissed
With Vision Divine

If the Universe provides
You with a lover,
Make love! Enjoy!
Unite with the Divine
And if the Universe shows you
You're to be alone,
Reflect! Enjoy!
Unite with the Divine

— for —

The greatest blessing
Of all in love is that
It's always ever
Within us
We're man and woman
Old and young
The union is ever
Within us

So
We don't have to hold on
    To anyone else
We don't need a lover
    To be in love
God takes care
    Of all His creatures
Even alone,
    We're never alone
Mother Nature takes care
    Of all Her creatures
Even alone,
    We're always all one

An exercise

Practice seeing the beauty in everyone . . . and the beauty in yourself . . . .

Every lover, every friend, everyone you meet, even everyone you see has their own unique beauty . . . their own unique face of God or spark of the divine which they reflect.

Can you see it?

Every lover you've ever had and ever will have has been a divine being, in their essence, in their true being . . . . Can you see it?

Their bodies are miraculous creations of a loving divine force, and by loving them you have united with that force . . . . And the most beautiful part of all is that the same is true for them, because they see the divinity in you.

A meditation for love-making

Do you want to create the perfect lover? Or become the perfect lover? Try a meditation similar to the following:

> *Sit, or lie down, so that you are very comfortable. Take a breath, exhale, and relax your body.... Take another breath, exhale, and relax your mind.... Take another breath, exhale, and let everything go.... Do this a few times until you are comfortably relaxed....*
>
> *Then picture yourself meeting your perfect lover. Picture yourself touching. Picture yourself possessing all of the qualities you desire. Picture yourself making love, easily and effortlessly and exquisitely.*
>
> *Affirm something like this (find affirmations which feel good to you):*
>
> *My ideal lover has come to me, easily and effortlessly.*
>
> *I am open and spontaneous — a perfectly satisfying lover!*
>
> *I now am the perfect lover, with my perfect lover.*

Take a moment or two to enjoy your fantasy. It will soon manifest for you, and it will be for the highest good of all concerned.

To be alone is to tune into the sacred being of yourself.

VI

Being Alone

Being alone and enjoying it is a fine art which is nearly a lost art in America today. A recent poll found that being alone was one of the major fears of people in this country. It's too bad, because being alone is one of the greatest opportunities for growth and creativity that there is.

Look at the great visionaries of history. Their visions, their true understanding, came in their moments of aloneness. To be alone is to tune into the sacred being of yourself.

If you enjoy being alone, you are well on your way to discovering deep personal freedom. If you don't enjoy being alone, there are several things you can do to change it. You're inevitably going to be alone some of the time, anyway, so you might as well learn to enjoy it.

Self-examination

One of the most powerful techniques is simply self-examination. Look directly — without avoiding *anything* — at all the things which you fear or feel uncomfortable about being alone. Look at what is going through your mind when you are alone. Do it in a way that respects yourself, without judgment or guilt. But clearly see all the things you tell yourself. Pay attention to the thoughts, and the songs, and anything else that goes through your mind.

Watch your thoughts and feelings. That's all that's necessary to do. Watch them arise, observe them when they dominate your consciousness, and let them go. Notice that these thoughts and feelings do pass — all things pass. And they pass much more quickly if you are free to observe them, clearly and openly, without rejecting them.

The self-questioning process

If you are having any difficulty when you're alone, go through the self-questioning process which was described in Chapter II ('A tantric practice'). Ask yourself, "What am I feeling?" or, "What am I telling myself?" Tell yourself the first answer that pops into your head, and then say "Thank you!" to yourself. Then ask it again, and again, if necessary, as many times as you need to until you get an answer that feels good to you.

Keep trying deeper and deeper questions, until you find the question and the answer which dissolve your difficulties. There's no need to fear being alone. You are an infinitely creative being — and it is usually much easier to tap into your full creative potential when you're alone than when you're with others.

A meditation on being alone

When you're alone, you are open to receiving the guidance of your own intuitive mind. A meditation such as the following can help you to do this:

> *Sit comfortably. Take a while to relax your body, and your mind, and your whole being.*
>
> *Pick some affirmations that feel good to you, and say them repeatedly, with emotion. Some suggestions:*
>
> *I enjoy being alone.*
>
> *Within my solitude, I am discovering deep understanding.*
>
> *Every day, in every way, my life is getting better and better.*
>
> *My intuitive understanding is complete, clear, and ever present.*
>
> *I am open to receiving everything I need to know, and everything I need to have.*

Enjoy your time alone. There are deep teachings within these special moments — if you give yourself time to hear your own inner intuitive teacher.*

---

* One activity which can be very valuable when you're alone is to listen to cassette tapes which are uplifting and inspiring, or deeply relaxing. Whatever Publishing has produced some fine meditation tapes, including "Stress Reduction and Creative Meditations" by Marcus Allen, and "Creative Visualization" by Shakti Gawain.

By focusing primarily on your short-range needs, you can lose your long-range sight . . . . Focus on your highest purpose in life, your deepest wishes, your most exquisite dreams . . . .

VII

Work

Buckminster Fuller says he realized when he was a young man that it was no longer necessary to work for a living, for we have reached a level of automation and productivity which no longer requires that everyone must labor for their sustenance. So he spent several years looking at what needed to be done for humankind, and for the planet in general. He followed his intuition and his dreams, and proceeded to make one of the most important contributions of the century.

Look at your beliefs

Look at your beliefs about work — are they limiting your personal freedom? So many people have never even asked themselves this question — and it is a question which could transform the qualities of their lives.

Our beliefs form the foundation which create our experience of the world. If we believe we must work for

40 hours a week, doing something we dislike or consider menial or uncreative, we will find that the world will support our belief, and it will seem to us as if it is essential for us to continue working in order to provide even just the bare necessities of life. But it's very important to realize that this is just merely one kind of belief (an all-too popular one, however), and that many other people have operated very successfully with different belief systems.

Examine your beliefs and understand that they can be changed, if you find that you have beliefs (even deep, core beliefs) that do not serve your highest purpose.

Affirmations are powerful tools for changing even the deepest, core beliefs. If you're not satisfied with your present belief structure, find the affirmations which will change it.

The single, most powerfully motivating force which keeps many people in jobs they dislike is insecurity — fear of not having enough, fear of not making it without working at that job. Affirm your fears away. Remember that when you are following your intuitive guidance and acting for your highest good the universe will always take care of you — you will always have enough.

I left a very secure, full-time job to start a very insecure publishing business, which proceeded to lose (or rather, outflow) a great deal of money in its first three years of existence. Leaving that secure, regularly paying job was not easy — it took a leap, a leap of faith. But I knew that I was compromising with myself, compromising with my full potential, by continuing that job. And I knew that the universe would support me — though I didn't know how. And it has, as it always does. I'm not rich, because I haven't visualized it clearly for myself —

at least not yet. But I do live in abundance, comfortably, with a lifestyle which allows me to work for myself when and only when I feel like working, and which gives me plenty of time for my creative projects.

You can do the same — if you wish.

Your highest purpose

Most people work in order to survive. And this takes so much time and energy that they neglect their deepest desires and their greatest areas of creativity. By focusing primarily on your short-term needs — food, rent or mortgage payments, clothes, dental and medical bills, etc. — you can lose your long-range sight.

Start instead by focusing on your highest purpose in life, your deepest wishes, your most exquisite dreams. Then find or create work which is in alignment with these things, and you will find that the details of your life will start to fall into place as you align yourself more and more with your highest purpose. This can take some time to unfold, but it is a journey well worth making.

Your ideal

Some people have difficulty discovering their highest purpose. It has been so long since we have taken the time and energy to focus on our purposes that we've forgotten what they are. Right now, take the time to play this little game — which is powerful enough to create profound changes in your life — called "Your Ideal Scene."

Take a sheet of paper, if you are alone, or sit down with a close friend. Pretend that you are suddenly five or ten years in the future, and that you have managed to create everything your heart has ever desired for yourself. Allow yourself to be completely fanciful and unrealistic. You have succeeded beyond your wildest dreams.

Describe where you live, what you do, how much money you make, what kind of relationships you have, etc. Be as thorough as you can.

Play with this, just like a child plays at being what they want to be when they grow up. If you could have anything you want, what would it be?

Have fun with this exercise. Allow your fantasies to wander, and explore all kinds of different possibilities, if you feel like it. This isn't 'just child's play' — it could have a very concrete effect on your future.

Now that you have explored your ideal scene, now that you have taken your dreams out of the closet, you are in the right state of mind to phrase — in a short, simple paragraph — your highest purpose in life. And you have the proper perspective to sketch out both long-term and short-term goals for yourself.

Take fifteen minutes, do the above exercise, and the one which follows:

Take a sheet of paper and write, "My highest purpose in life is..." and complete the sentence. Use no more than one short paragraph to express what it is. Of course, it will be in broad, general terms.

Then, under that paragraph, list every

*goal — both long-term and short-term —
which is in alignment with that purpose,
which helps to further that purpose.*

*Some will be very general, some more
specific. Underneath the goals — perhaps on
separate sheets of paper, if necessary — list the
immediate steps necessary to accomplish that
goal.*

Every broad, general purpose can be broken down
into a series of general goals. Every general goal can be
broken down into several specific goals. Every specific
goal can be broken down into specific steps necessary to
accomplish that goal.

Keep focusing on these goals, and you can achieve
them. Don't ever fear being trapped by your goals, however — you can always change or delete your goals, if
and when you feel like it.

Once you have your highest purpose and your goals
clearly listed in front of you, you are in a much better
position to determine exactly what you want to do with
your valuable time and energy than you were before.
This is the key to finding what has been called 'right
livelihood' for yourself — that is, work which is in
alignment with your highest purpose and your goals.
This is the only kind of work which will be deeply
satisfying for you. This is the only work you will have
the kind of energy for which will cause you to truly
succeed, in whatever ways you wish. It may require a
leap of faith — in fact, it probably will — but you will
never regret making it.

A meditation to create your perfect work

As with everything else, it is essential to create a clear picture of success on inner planes before it can manifest on outer planes, in the so-called 'real world'. Try the following meditation, and watch the results:

Take a few minutes to relax. You can use either a short three-breath method to relax, or a longer method.

For the short method, if you just have a few minutes to do this exercise, simply take one deep breath and, as you exhale, affirm to yourself, "My body is now relaxing." Take another deep breath, and affirm to yourself as you exhale, "My mind is now relaxing." Take a final deep breath, and affirm to yourself as you exhale, "I am letting everything go" (or, "I am now totally relaxed").

For the longer method, if you have ten minutes or more for this exercise, simply take a breath and, as you exhale, relax your feet. Take another breath, and, as you exhale, relax your ankles. Continue a deep, rhythmic breathing, and as you exhale, move up through your entire body, letting each part go: calves, knees, thighs, buttocks, sexual organs, lower back, stomach, diaphragm, mid-back, heart, lungs, upper back, shoulders, upper arms, elbows, forearms, hands, neck, face, back of head, top of head . . . .

Now you're relaxed, deeply. Enjoy the feeling of your deep relaxation. Now you're ready for any of the meditations in this book.

Imagine yourself doing exactly the kind of work you most want to do. Try to actually see yourself doing it. If you can't see clearly, that's okay — but be sure to imagine it, creatively. Play with it, like a child. Have fun with it. Imagine how you spend your time. Imagine your work environment. Imagine getting paid for your work. Imagine yourself being very satisfied and happy with the work and its rewards. You don't even have to clearly see how to get from where you are at present to where you dream of going. Just consistently imagine the final situation, and the vast power of your unconscious will show you how to get there.

Follow the creative visualization with affirmations, such as:

> *"There is nothing to fear. All my fears are unfounded."*
>
> *"The Universe provides, abundantly."*
>
> *"My perfect, creative work comes to me, easily and effortlessly."*
>
> *"My connection with infinite intelligence shows me my perfect work and play in the world."*
>
> *"I am fulfilled as a creative being."*
>
> *"I am a success."*
>
> *"I can accomplish anything my heart desires."*

Make up any affirmations that seem appropriate to you.

Then, take a deep breath, and affirm to yourself, "This, or something better, is now

*manifesting for the highest good of all con-
cerned. So be it. So it is."*
    *Take one more deep breath, and, in your
own time and in your own way, return to your
waking consciousness.*

Do this daily for a short while. Soon — within three
weeks — you will be beginning to create a much more
effective work attitude and work situation. Soon you
will be given clear, insightful, creative ideas which will
transform your work into something which is totally in
alignment with your highest purpose in the world.
    Be persistent, but don't worry about how you will
achieve it. The means will become clear to you.

Enjoy your work

It is important to see, too, that whatever you are
now doing has its own perfect reason for being, and can
be satisfying in its own way. Very monotonous, routine
work, for example, is excellent for practice in 'mindful-
ness' — watching your thoughts, observing yourself.
Many people derive great satisfaction and fulfillment
from doing work which in itself is mundane, but which
serves others in their family or community.
    Enjoy your work — regardless of what you are do-
ing, and regardless of whether or not you desire to be
doing something else. You'll discover all kinds of new
rewards when you're able to do this.

We are as limited, or as unlimited, as we imagine ourselves to be.

VIII

Money

Now we're getting down to the bottom line.

Here's an excellent, yet brief, exercise to do — one which we've done at some of the workshops my friends and I have led. Take a few minutes, and do it! — the rest of the chapter will be far more meaningful for you personally if you do.

Take a piece of paper, and at the top of the paper, write "Money is . . ." and then underneath, list everything — good, bad, irrelevant, weird, embarrassing, whatever — that comes to mind about money. List the things you've heard about money. List the things you tell yourself about money. Just take about 10 minutes, and you'll probably get all the "biggies" down . . . or take a little longer if you feel like you're avoiding something.

This list — whatever you wrote — probably has a

lot of contradicting feelings and ideas on it. Now see if you can get this: *money is none of those things ...* money in itself is nothing at all, except what we make it. Money is really a very mystical thing. It is just a piece of paper, with some ink on it, some letters and numbers and designs on it — very similar to this page you are reading. And yet there are so many conflicting attitudes and feelings about it.

In itself, it has no value at all, but is simply a medium of exchange, a convention set up to assist people in trading one thing for another in an efficient way.

Look over your list again — look at how you feel and what you think about money. It is good, it is bad.... Can you see how these beliefs have created your present experience of your financial situation? Can you see that your beliefs about money are self-fulfilling? Can you see that you can have it any way you want it — if you change your beliefs?

We can have as much or as little money as we want. In fact, we *do* have as much or as little money as we want. This is explained by what I call my *"cool* theory": everyone affirms and therefore creates exactly the lifestyle that they think is "cool" — or right, or proper, or appropriate for them. The bum on the street, in the deepest levels of his being — even if he denies it consciously — thinks that being a bum is really the most appropriate thing for him to be. The way you're presently living your life is the way you think is best, or the way you feel you deserve, on your deepest levels of being. If you want to make changes in your life, you've got to change those deep inner beliefs, through your creative meditation and affirmation, through the power of your own imagination.

It is not necessary to struggle for money, or feel pressured by money. It is merely necessary to understand the principles by which it operates, and to make your own choice as to how much you want to create for yourself.

I am not a master of money — at least at this time. I have not created great riches for myself. But I have moved far beyond my past 'poverty consciousness' (which I thought was 'cool' in the 60s and early 70s), and I have created a life of abundance, based on a knowingness that the universe is supporting me, comfortably, wherever I go, whatever I do. This was relatively easy for me to create, by examining my core beliefs about money, about my lifestyle in general, and by changing these beliefs through creative meditation and affirmations. It's quite amazing to see how quickly your entire world can change, as a result of a small amount of effective inner work.

Limiting beliefs

Our experience of the world is created from our deepest core beliefs of ourselves and our world. This is a deep, powerful teaching, once you grasp it. Most people think that it works the other way around: the world is a certain way, and so we develop our 'realistic' beliefs as a result of what the world imposes on us. But I encourage you and challenge you to try this other view on for size, and see what happens.

What if it is true that our deepest beliefs create our experience of the world? If so, we should obviously take the time to examine these beliefs, and become familiar with them. This is not all that difficult, if we use the process of self-questioning described in Chapter II. And it is not all that difficult to discover where these beliefs came from — usually parents, peer groups, or others we respect or admire. Some of these beliefs are useful and supportive. Many are limiting and unnecessary. These can be changed — have no doubts about that.

You are in complete control of your life. Certainly no one else is! You are creating your own experience constantly, based on your core beliefs of what you are like, what you deserve, what the world is like, etc., and reflected constantly in your mind by what you are telling yourself.

Look at what you are telling yourself. Many people are simply not aware of their own thought processes. Focus on your thoughts, and observe them. Let the negative, limiting ones go. Focus instead on others that serve you better and that are closer to the reality you wish to create for yourself. Any thoughts of lack or limitation are unnecessary. You can do anything you like. You can create any kind of lifestyle you like. You can have as much money as you like — it's true, if you simply believe it to be true.

A very wise person (I'm not sure who) once said, "*Argue for your limitations, and they are yours.*" That's it, in a nutshell. We are as limited or as unlimited as we imagine ourselves to be. Let go of your limiting beliefs. Instead, imagine your greatness, and it is yours.

A creative meditation for money

Try the following meditation, and watch it produce some very tangible results — often in a very short time:

> *Get comfortable, close your eyes . . . .*
> *Relax, in any way you wish . . . .*

Imagine money coming to you, in any way that feels good to you. You can simply feel it as an energy which you are attracting. Or you can see it as green bills, or as checks. Imagine it coming from one direction, then another, then another. Imagine it coming from every direction. Move around the entire circle of every possible direction.

Feel the abundance of the universe showering you with money.

Affirm, with energy, words such as:

"I am open to receiving the blessings of an abundant universe."

"Money comes to me, easily and effortlessly."

"My income exceeds my expenses."

"I am a source of abundance in an abundant universe."

"My connection with infinite intelligence is now yielding me a vast personal fortune."

As you are saying the last affirmation, imagine your mind connected with a focal point of energy in the universe which is showering you with wealth and abundance.

Try this meditation daily for a week or so, and watch for some very pleasant things to come your way. I often do this meditation in the morning, lying on my back in bed, along with a visualization of perfect health, and of effortlessly accomplishing whatever creative projects or business affairs lie before me. Once it's handled on the inner plane, the outer plane often seems to take place all by itself, without much effort. Opportunities arise, as if by magic, and you find yourself equipped to take full advantage of them.

Once you're doing the meditation, become aware of the fact that you are conditioning your powerful and vast subconscious to receive even a greater good in the form of growth and health, etc. Your subconscious will respond, in its own way, by giving you certain ideas, suggestions, 'hunches'. Follow up on these ideas, even if they seem impulsive. If they feel right to you, many will be very fruitful. And if they aren't fruitful, nothing has been lost, because a great deal of experience has been gained.

Creating abundance

It can be very liberating, personally and financially, to understand that creating money and creating abundance are often two very different things — and abundance is relatively easy to create. Many people who have a substantial amount of money still have not created a feeling of abundance for themselves, and they are often worried about inflation, taxes, investments, the future, etc. And yet there are people with very little money who have a feeling of abundance, and who live in a world where there is always more than enough of everything. For *abundance is a state of mind* — a state of mind which can consciously be created by you, with the power of your mind.

We live in an abundant universe: look at the number of stars in the sky — 100 billion known galaxies, with an average of 200 billion suns each — look at the number of seeds on an oak, or a eucalyptus tree, or a dandelion. We are surrounded by infinite abundance, if we stop cutting ourselves off from it, open up to it, and let ourselves be a part of it.

Start seeing yourself, right now, as an abundant being. It doesn't matter whether you've got a bank account of a certain size. The only thing that matters is your state of mind — which is reflected by the things you are telling yourself. Start telling yourself that you are an abundant being, in an abundant universe, with plenty for everybody. So be it — so it is.

The ten-percent plan

I have developed a system of money management which is working very well for me, and which I have recommended to many others. Much of this was inspired by Leonard Orr, from his book *Rebirthing In the New Age.*

A very common problem with many people is that they tend to spend whatever they make. This was true with me until about four years ago. Even when I worked at a job in which I saw regular and dramatic salary increases, I still kept spending whatever I earned.

Then, I started saving ten percent of my income — in effect, tithing it to myself. I realized that, if I always had enough with whatever amount of money I was making, I would always have enough just spending ninety percent of the money I was making. At first my savings didn't seem to amount to much — but after about six months, it suddenly felt like a sizeable amount, and then I put it into a long-term savings account, at a much higher interest rate.

It started feeling so good to save ten percent that I soon began saving twenty percent: I set up two different accounts, and put ten percent into savings, which I vowed not to touch, no matter what, and I put the other ten percent into an investment account, which I was free to play with and invest in anything I felt like. I decided to invest half of that account into my own business and my own creativity — and have used it when needed, buying instruments and equipment, and printing books and pressing albums of my music when I couldn't find other sources of funding. But the other half goes to other things, such as silver, stocks, and my friends' creative ideas.

My yearly income isn't that impressive — I run my own business, and live off my royalties. But after a year or so, these accounts grew enough to make me start feeling like quite an abundant entrepreneur. I took another step, and started putting away another ten percent into another account, which I call my "large purchases" account. This allows me to have the cash for larger purchases or unexpected expenses without dipping into my savings or investment accounts. Now I'm living on 70 percent of what I make, and the other 30 percent is working for my present and future enjoyment.

I recommend starting by saving just ten percent, then increasing it. If, during some weeks, you can't save as much as you are intending to, don't worry about it — nothing is lost. But just the fact that you have set up a framework in which you save, invest, and buy large purchases and still have money to cover your other expenses will assist you in expanding your concepts of the amount of money you need to create. And you'll either create more of it, or you'll use what you now have more wisely.

Some people have asked me why bother to save money when the rate of inflation is greater than the rate of interest earned? But I feel that it's better to have something saved than nothing at all. And the game to play with at least some of your investment account money is to try to put it into things that will increase in value faster than the rate of inflation.

We don't have to worry about inflation, incidentally, and we don't have to worry about recession or depression either. We live in an abundant universe, and if we have this core belief, we will always create enough for ourselves and our families. And in so doing, we will be able to assist others around us in overcoming their negative conditioning through our positive example. Some people made fortunes during the so-called 'great depression' — the prosperous ones were those who refused to believe in what the newspapers and everyone else kept believing, and used their creative imaginations to tap into the abundance of the universe, which is available for any and all of us.

To sum it up

A great master once said

Ask and you shall receive.

Ask for the money, the lifestyle, the things you deserve and want in your heart. Ask for it in your daily life, whenever appropriate. Ask for it in meditation — visualize it coming to you. Ask, and you shall receive — this is a law of the universe, reflecting the power of the creative word. Try it, and you'll see.

You are a creative being. Know it. Accept it. Enjoy it. There are infinite possibilities . . . and you're dreaming of them every day.

IX

Creativity

Our culture has been very progressive and success-ful in some ways — and an abysmal failure in others. One of the greatest failures of our educational systems involves creativity. Every child is a creative genius. Children draw, sing, dance, make up stories and songs, make up imaginary friends, play incredibly fanciful games and do all kinds of other very creative things with abandon. They are connected with their intuition, which is the source of all creativity.

Then, unfortunately, we send these children to school to "learn." In all too many instances, their natural intuitive spontaneity is ignored and even de-nied, and they are forced to sit behind uncomfortable desks for six hours a day while they are drilled con-stantly into believing that education is the accumula-tion of a huge amount of rational 'facts'. The schools teach the children that they are stupid, because they don't know all these facts. Their natural creative genius is not reinforced, and all too often, withers away.

I was considered a bright, successful student. But I secretly felt that I didn't know anything — I felt the only thing I learned in school was how to impress teachers rather than how to truly learn and grow. I have a feeling that most students, whether successful or not, essentially learn from school — on a deep, perhaps 'subconscious' level — that they don't know much of anything, that they are basically stupid and uncreative. At least, that was my experience.

Getting a 'higher education' was, for me, even worse. I was primarily interested in theater and English — two very creative fields. Perhaps my experience would have been different if I had been a Business Administration major, or a Physical Education major. I hope so. Because the things I supposedly 'learned' at the University caused me to shut down, rather than open up, my creative potential even more.

In English classes, we analyzed other people's writings to the point where very few of us felt we could write anything. Poetry seemed so complex — because of the teachers' detailed, rational analysis of every phrase — that I felt I would never be capable of creating any poetry. It was far too dense and difficult.

Outwardly, I appeared to be a success in school — I graduated 'phi beta kappa' and 'magna cum laude' amidst all kinds of obsolete ceremony and speeches. But inwardly, I was dry, shut down, and cynical — this was the result of my higher education!

It wasn't until six years after I left the University that I was able to write anything. And unfortunately I've found many others in creative fields who've had a similar experience. After a period of time, though, I finally forgot the teachers and the analysis, and I gradually became able to write again. It took me six years, but I was able to connect with my own innate creativity again.

I'm not saying that there aren't any good high schools and universities. I'm simply relating my experience. There are many people who have had a very different experience in school, fortunately. But whether your experience was good or bad doesn't really matter in the long run: you can become as creative as you want to be.

Unlocking your creative genius

Every person is a creative genius, potentially. Perhaps you can't accept that statement — perhaps you feel, like so many others, that the word 'genius' should be reserved for a chosen few, such as Einstein and Bach and Buckminster Fuller and any others you feel have gone far beyond the accomplishments of most people. But I use 'genius' in a broader sense: I feel that a genius is one who is connected with his or her intuitive nature, intuitive senses. Everyone has this intuitive sense, and we're using it all the time. We simply need to become more aware of what we're naturally doing all the time, and in doing so we will unlock a genius within us. Our creativity will open up, easily and effortlessly, and poetry, books, music, crafts, skills, and all kinds of other satisfying creative things will spring from us, spontaneously.

There are many different ways to unlock the creative genius within you. One is by remembering and reconnecting with the fantasies, dreams, and activities you experienced as a child. Children know exactly where their greatest creative potential lies. What did you dream of doing and being? What did you actually do when you were young? Remember it, connect with it, and *act* on it. Get out your old crayons, or sit down and write something, or start making something — whatever you have an impulse to do. You'll never regret it.

Another way to open up your creativity is to tune into your deepest dreams and fantasies that have kept surfacing for you all your life. What creative things do you imagine yourself doing? I deeply feel that *imagining* doing something takes you halfway toward its completion. Take writing a book, for example. Just the fact that you imagine yourself writing that particular book, and that you imagine the title and the general structure, means that you are not only completely capable of doing it, but it also means that the book is half written already! And it's the most important half — the visionary half. The second half is relatively easy. Without the initial vision, nothing would be accomplished. Don't underestimate the power of your fantasies and daydreams! Within them is the power to create whatever your heart desires.

Perhaps the most powerful method of all of opening up your creativity is through meditation and affirmations. We'll get to that in a moment — but first, let's deal with the obstacles to unlocking the creative forces within you.

Let go of the judge

What is blocking your natural flow of creativity? For most people, the greatest obstacles to creativity — and to personal freedom in general — are the internal and external judges we have created for ourselves, and the negative self-image which these judgments have produced. Throughout our formative childhood and our 'education', we had many other people judging our activities and capabilities. Unconsciously, we gave these judges the power to affect us. As a result, we felt inadequate and guilty in many ways — and our creative channels dried up.

Let go of all judgments of yourself! Both those that come from within you, and those that other people give you. Don't give these judgments the power to affect you. Understand on a deep level that they are not serving you — unless, of course, those judgments happen to be totally positive and supportive. Whenever you find that you are critically judging yourself, simply let go of that thought, and replace it with something more supportive, such as, "I am a highly creative person," or "I am connected with my intuitive intelligence."

I have a friend who is a highly successful writer. He once told me that one of his fondest and deepest childhood memories was of his mother tucking him into bed at night. Every night she told him, "There's nothing you can't do in your life — you can do and be anything you want!" With early conditioning like that, no wonder he was successful. Whenever we find that we're being hard on ourselves, we should give ourselves some positive encouragement instead, just like my friend's mother.

Another great and unnecessary obstacle is the fear of failure. This too can be let go of — there is no need to fear failure at all. All our fears are unfounded, and failure is no exception. There is no such thing as failure, anyway: every 'failure' is merely another lesson to be learned on the way to your success — if you see it that way. The trial and error process is our natural process of growth — just as a child learning to walk has to fall down repeatedly as he or she is learning. If we made every fall significant, we'd still be sitting in our cribs.

Look at all the truly great people of history. Most of them have experienced many so-called "failures" before achieving success. They didn't give others the power to judge them, and they didn't fear failure.

Give yourself as much support and encouragement as you give to a child who you love who is doing something new and fresh — like taking a first step. You deserve just as much praise and support in your first creative steps — no matter how small they may seem.

Whether you want to dance, write, paint, start a business — *whatever* — give yourself permission to do it without judging yourself, especially at first. You can't write a book and critically edit it at the same time — which is often what people try to do. Write it first — even if it's just an extremely rough draft — without judging or editing in any way. Once you have finished your first draft — once you have taken your first steps — you can edit it and change it, applying your own and others' ideas for improving it.

A 15-minute exercise

Take fifteen minutes (or, if that's too confronting, take ten, or even five) to give yourself some time to open up your creativity. Just decide that you'll spend this time doing something new and creative, something you've dreamed of doing, perhaps, but somehow have never gotten around to doing it. Just sit there, and do whatever pops into your mind. Give yourself total freedom to do anything: write a poem . . . make up a song . . . sing something . . . play something . . . make something . . . invent something . . . imagine something . . . change something around . . . .

Do it now! Don't wait till tomorrow. One woman

who came to a workshop I gave said she had been intending *for years* to write poetry, but never got around to it, because she kept telling herself that she had to have everything together and organized in her life before she could write her poetry. She had been promising herself that she would start writing as soon as she cleaned out her entire house, even including her closets, and somehow she never got around to finishing that task. In a way, many of us are doing similar things with our creative energy — finding all kinds of absurd ways to postpone expressing ourselves. The woman in the workshop simply looked at what she was doing, decided it was unnecessary to wait until her closets were organized before writing poetry, and made a commitment to herself that she would write her first poem within two days. It worked. She may have a book out next. What if Shakespeare or Emily Dickenson had waited until *their* closets were clean? We'd be missing some great writing.

A tantric musician

I once lived in a little cottage on the grounds of an old mansion. There were several little cottages around, tucked in the woods. In one lived an older man who rarely came outside — I saw him only once or twice in several months and thought he was a hermit of some kind. A friend of mine saw him one day, sitting in the afternoon sun near his cottage. She got to talking with him, and asked him what he did. He said he was a musician, and he invited her in to hear him play.

She went into his place — it was dark and cluttered. One entire wall was covered with stacks of newspapers, piled over six feet high. All kinds of sticks had been jammed into the newspapers, and hanging on the sticks were objects of all kinds — pie tins, pot covers, cups, all sorts of things which would make a sound when struck. He picked up two spoons and started playing the objects on the wall. Then he handed her some spoons, and they played together. She loved it! She had never played anything before, but suddenly she was an instant musician, and got right into it.

Why not? There have been nights when several of us have gotten into playing our kitchen — banging on pots and pans and stoves and refrigerators and everything else around . . . .

When you're free, you're free to do whatever you feel like doing. Don't judge yourself for it. Just get into it, and enjoy it.

A meditation for opening up creativity

Give the following creative meditation a try. Make up your own variations to assist you with your own particular forms of creative expression.

> *Sit or lie comfortably. Close your eyes, and relax . . . .*
>
> *Imagine in whatever way feels good to you that you are a channel for the creative energy of the universe. Imagine being an open vessel, and having creative energy flowing through you.*
>
> *Imagine yourself doing specific things, things you dream of doing. For example, see the book you've wanted to write being completed, easily and effortlessly. Imagine how it will look when it's printed and bound. Imagine holding it in your hands and admiring it,*

feeling very pleased.

Take a fantasy journey, and see yourself as a master of whatever art or craft or business you wish. See yourself doing the things you want to do. See people appreciating you and supporting you abundantly in your creative expression.

Affirm to yourself words such as:

"I am an open channel of creativity."

"I am an open channel for exquisite, end-lessly abundant creativity, in many, many forms."

"Creativity comes to me, easily and ef-fortlessly."

"I am connected with my intuitive mind."

"My intuitive awareness is easily surfac-ing, opening up all my creative chan-nels."

"_____ (say the name of your creative project) is completed, easily and effortlessly."

"I am connected to the master within me."

Make up your own affirmations.

Then, take a deep breath, and come out of your meditative relaxation. Take a moment to enjoy your creation, and to appreciate your creative energy.

All creation begins from within. Have fun with this exercise. Start right now enjoying your own creativity. This is certainly one of the best methods of cultivating it.

Some good advice

I have a good friend named John Donahue. He came into Minneapolis, Minnesota, from a small town when he was 18 years old, and started directing little children's plays. Many people told him he should go to the University to study theater, but he said that the University only knows how to teach people to *teach* theater — and the only way to learn how to do anything is to *do* it. He started by building a tiny stage in a shabby, abandoned firehouse building in the slums. Today, he is the director of a vast, multi-million dollar theater complex known all over the world.

He once told me something which has stuck with me, and which has been very useful for unlocking creativity — and for enjoying life in general. I was acting for him, and was having some trouble with the role; I went to him and began to try to explain my difficulties. He just looked at me and said, "Cut the shit and do the thing."

I've never forgotten those words. They have helped me cut through a great deal of garbage and lame excuses which over the years had been blocking my natural creative expression.

You too are a creative being. Know it. Accept it. Enjoy it. There are infinite possibilities ... and you're dreaming of them every day.

"When people make their thoughts pure, all their food is pure."

—James Allen
As a Man Thinketh

X

Food and Drink

There is a long poem from the Chinese tradition of Buddhism called "Shodoka," written in the 8th century A.D. One verse of it goes like this:

Release your hold on earth, water, fire, wind
Drink and eat as you wish in the Nirvana
mind
All things are transient and completely empty –
This is the great Enlightenment of the Buddha.

The introduction of natural foods into mainstream America which has occurred over the past decade has been a very beneficial thing, for the most part. Our rates of heart disease are decreasing, for example, as Americans are eating more whole foods, less meat, and exercising more.

But our interest in natural foods has been a mixed blessing — for with it has come an awareness which leads to some very negative conditioning for many people, and to downright fanaticism for some people. Many people are now affirming to themselves and their children that sugar, white flour, salt, meat, coffee, alcohol — and even in some cases eggs and dairy products — are harmful, poisonous substances. Many people are creating massive guilt for themselves every time they have an ice cream cone or a candy bar. They're telling children they're going to have cavities, and they're going to get sick. Unfortunately, these things — like any other affirmations of both a positive and negative nature — tend to become self-fulfilling prophesies if they are repeated often enough.

It is far more important what you tell yourself, what you think and say about your eating habits, than what you actually eat and drink. It is certainly true that some food is better for your body than other food. My stomach usually feels more content after a bowl of yogurt than after a meal of canned corn beef hash. My body clearly tells me what it wants and doesn't want. So does yours. Trust your body, and don't listen to your head, whenever it's telling you that what you're eating is bad for you.

I was a vegetarian for five years. It was very good for my body, and I was generally healthy. But I was also impossible to live with. I couldn't stand the sight or smell of meat, and felt that people who ate it were obviously on a far lower level of consciousness than I was. I was a health food chauvinist. Then I met a certain Tibetan *lama* — or teacher — who literally glowed with radiant health, and who loved meat, especially greasy, fried meat, and never ate his vegetables. He laughed at people's food fetishes. He taught me many things, and one of those things was to eat and enjoy whatever you want to, without being neurotic about it.

Now I eat and drink whatever I wish when I wish. I play a game with myself of waiting until I'm good and hungry, then eating exactly what my body wants — not what my head wants, and not what my mouth wants, but what my whole body wants. My rhythm is probably different from yours, but I tend to wait until fairly late in the day, usually, and then eat one substantial meal. I drink orange juice and coffee in the morning, and I'll often drink beer in the evening. And I affirm that all of it is very good for my body.

A tantric experiment

During one period in my life when I was meditating a lot and attempting to do without a sustained romantic relationship, I got passionately into white sugar. Every afternoon, I would go to my favorite donut shop and have a huge, gloppy, sugary mess. I looked forward to it intensely, and enjoyed it immensely. But I would leave with a feeling of not being fulfilled — and so I knew something was going on. It wasn't the sugar I was craving, it was something else — like love and affection. But my sugar fetish persisted, to the point where I was spending a lot of time and going way out of my way to feed my sugar habit.

I decided to do something about it, and considered several possibilities, from cold turkey to over-indulgence. Then I decided to try a tantric experiment. I went to my favorite donut shop and ordered *four* huge gloppy sweet things, and a cup of coffee. I ate every one of them, and ordered three more, and another cup of coffee. The woman behind the counter looked at me as if I was totally crazy. And, in a way, she was right — but there was a method to my madness. I started into the second batch, when suddenly my body started screaming (inwardly, to myself — not outwardly, fortunately) *"Stop! Enough! Yuck! This is crazy!"* So I left, feeling somewhat nauseous and buzzy from all that sugar and coffee.

The next day I felt absolutely no desire for sweets of any kind. In fact, I've eaten very little sugar ever since. By plunging into the center of the poison, I effectively cleaned up a neurotic pattern. I don't reject sugar — for myself or others. I can take it or leave it. But I'm no longer craving it.

You are not what you eat

By taking our eating so seriously, and by telling each other "you are what you eat," we're denying ourselves not only a lot of enjoyment, but we're denying our body's incredible strength and natural cleansing and healing functions. We are much more than what we eat. We are physical beings with bodies that heal themselves; we are emotional beings with feelings that guide us intuitively, and tell us what to do; we are mental beings, with the power to create our bodies and our life experience through our mind's creative energies; and we are spiritual beings, one with everyone, united on the deepest levels of our being with the whole Universe. We are much more than what we eat.

Padma Sambhava — the great mystic who brought Buddhism to Tibet — drank huge doses of poison several times during his lifetime. It never affected him at all — he understood that mind is more powerful than body, and that we can only be poisoned if we allow ourselves to be. If his body could handle large doses of poison, certainly your body can handle whatever you put into it — unless you are very extreme, and unless you ignore your body's communications to you about what it wants.

I'm not suggesting that you use this kind of thinking — the tantric perspective — as an excuse for abusing your body in any way. If you're not healthy, your body is giving you messages, telling you what you need to eat and drink and do in order to be healthy again; if you're overweight, you need to eat less, and/or exercise a lot more.

Love your body, trust your body, and give it what it wants. And it will serve you well.

A meditation

Relax, take some deep breaths, close your eyes . . . .

See and feel your body in perfect, radiant health. Feel the life energy pouring through you, cleansing and healing you.

Affirm the following:

"My body is perfectly healthy."

"My body is perfectly pure and healthy."

"I always tune into my body and eat exactly what's best for me."

"Whatever I eat is good for me."

So be it — so it is!

*Transformation is here and now —
it happens in the present moment,
not in the past or future.*

XI

Meditation and Yoga

Meditation and yoga are excellent for you — physically, emotionally, mentally, and spiritually — but, like everything else, they too can turn into addictions and other neurotic behavior. Don't ever put yourself down because you can't meditate or you aren't meditating enough or you missed your yoga session. That's using a good tool for a bad effect.

After many years of experience, I'm quite familiar with both the benefits and the pitfalls of meditation and yoga. Many of the practices are excellent for Westerners, and many of the practices create as much or more neurosis than they dissolve.

The benefits

Physically, your body can be healed and strengthened through meditation and yoga. I'm convinced that regular physical yoga exercises can help to avoid a large number of expensive doctor and hospital bills. Meditation connects you with your body, and allows you to become very sensitive to its tensions, its energy, its state of health. And physical forms of yoga can correct a great many physical problems you may have, and prevent others.

In fact, simple, silent meditation in itself purifies and heals your body over a period of time. I first heard this said by an old Zen master, named Katsuki Sekida (author of the fine book, *Zen Training*). He said that many people wouldn't believe it yet, but he insisted it was true. I believe it, for it has been true in my experience.

Emotionally, meditation and yoga have a wonderful effect. They calm emotion, without repressing. You usually feel good after meditating and/or doing yoga. Even if you're in a time of emotional turmoil, a grounding in meditation and yoga practice can give you a healthy psychic distance from your emotions, so that your whole experience becomes less intense, less important and serious.

Yet also, even more importantly, meditation can tune you into your feelings in a way which is clarifying, and ultimately even enlightening — through meditation you can grow to understand that your emotions are a very important part of your experience, something to be embraced, and something from which you can learn a great deal about yourself. For within our emotions are the doors to our intuitive understanding — the source of our knowledge, power, and enlightenment.

Mentally, meditation and yoga also have a very positive effect. They can clarify and simplify difficult problems or decisions. They calm a rampant rational mind: if you happen to be going on and on about something excessively, without a satisfying resolution, a simple quiet period of meditation can give you a distance from your thought processes, and cause you to put it in a much clearer perspective. Often a simple solution will appear without any effort at all.

Meditation helps you to stop identifying so completely with your thoughts, and your feelings, and your body. You come to realize that you are something beyond all of these things — for these things are changing all the time. There is a deeper, more constant thread which runs through your entire being. For lack of better words, we can call it your spiritual nature, or your divine essence.

Spiritually, meditation and yoga have their greatest effect, for they can give you the deep knowledge of who you really are. You are, in reality, one with everything, an integral part of the Universe. On the spiritual level of understanding — the highest plane of knowledge — there is no distinction between things, for all things are all the same substance, which is pure energy, at their core. You are one with a blade of grass, a tree, a star. You are the life energy of the Universe. You are endlessly being nourished by this energy... you are eternally being reborn.

The pitfalls

The pitfalls of meditation and yoga can be summed up in a very useful rule of thumb, which is to be applied to any and all psychological or spiritual theories and practices:

> *If it dissolves neuroses, it is good for you. If (or when) it starts creating more neuroses*

than it dissolves, let it go. It is time to move on
to something else.

The most brilliant teachings in the world, like our greatest scientific discoveries, can be either skillfully used or unskillfully misused. It's up to you to discover within your own understanding whether the practices you are doing are solving problems or creating them. Don't be afraid to move on to new experiences if your heart is telling you that you can grow more by trying something else.

Meditation

Meditation can take many different forms, ranging from the totally passive meditation of silence — where you simply sit, or lie down, and let all thoughts go, until you are eventually in a state of complete, wordless, wonderful silence — to very active forms such as visualization and affirmations, which are given throughout this book.

Take some time to do some meditation . . . some silent practices . . . some stress-reducing relaxation . . . some magic . . . some creative visualization . . . whatever you want to call it, whatever you want to do.

Do it slowly . . . take your time . . . and make your connections, each in your own way, with your inner truth . . . your infinite intelligence.

If we take the time, now, to do this well, we will make a connection in this moment which is forever with us, at our call, effortlessly . . . .

Transformation is here and now. It hap-

pens in the present moment, not in the past or future.

Silence

Take some time to just sit in silence . . . .

It may prove to be a unique opening for you — something which you can never experience through words. Take two minutes, or half an hour, or an hour — whatever you want.

> *Just sit or lie very comfortably. Take some time to relax your body and mind by consciously letting go of any tension you discover in your body/mind. Then simply sit in silence. As thoughts arise, simply let them go. Don't anticipate anything. Just sit in silence.*

The experiences of this type of meditation are very different for each person. At some times, there may be instant insights, beyond words . . . deep experiences . . . experiences of energy moving through you. At some times, difficult problems may dissolve with simple solutions.

At other times, it may seem as if nothing happens at all . . . . And then, months or even years later, you may realize the value that you gained from that moment of just sitting in silence.

There are many different approaches to finding the silence within:

A Zen approach:

Sit there and do nothing and find your own way.

A Tibetan approach:

Find the silence between your thoughts, and stay in that silence for a while.

A Tibetan teacher used to say, "Look into the space between your thoughts . . . what is the space between your thoughts?"

A traditional Buddhist approach:

When you experience a thought, say to yourself, "That was a thought," and then let it go. Don't judge it, don't reject it, don't dwell on it, just let it go, and return to your meditation.

At first it may seem as if you are inundated, overwhelmed with a vast number of thoughts rushing in . . . . But keep at it, and you will soon be rewarded with an experience of silence . . . or of fulfillment . . . or of discovery. You may even experience the complete perfection of yourself, and of every moment of your life.

Why not give it a try? It might be more rewarding than watching television.

The active forms of meditation

Now I want to share with you some of the more active forms of meditation, which involve visualization, and have been especially effective for me. Don't worry if you can't 'visualize' clearly. Simply imagine it, feel it, and keep your attention on it. Even if your inner vision is so shimmering, so light that it is hardly there at all, even so it has great power. The vaguest shimmerings can live on in your memory, in your subconscious, with as much meaning as the clearest vision.

In the deepest sense, you are 'visualizing' all the time, in your mind, in your imagination.

These active forms of meditation constitute the essence of true magic, for they can, with repeated use, focus our creative minds in a way that deeply influences the power of our subconscious. And once our subconscious mind has been given the instructions to create something, it can and will do it — for our subconscious connects us with the forces of creation. We are all creative beings. And we can have whatever we truly want, if we but understand these principles, and apply them repeatedly.

I urge you to experiment with some of the following active meditations, and see how they feel. If nothing else, do the 'creative meditation', and see if it produces some surprising results for you!

The initial meditations will prepare you to expand, and to increase your good and your power in the world.

Pillar of light

Here's a fifteen-minute exercise which prepares your body and mind to go beyond all imagined limitations:

> *Sit comfortably... relax.... (Pause whenever there are dots... and take a moment to absorb it.) Close your eyes, take sev-*

*eral deep breaths, and relax more deeply . . . .
Enjoy the feeling – it feels very good to relax
deeply . . . . Now imagine that your spine is a
beautiful, shimmering, blue, energy field . . . .
Energy flows up it and down it, and it is light,
and healing . . . it dissolves all tensions . . . .*

*The pillar has an opening at the bottom —
at the base of your spine (or at the soles of your
feet, if you're lying down). This opening sends
that energy deeply into the Earth . . . and the
Earth sends energy up through that opening,
from its greatest depths — right from the
center of the Earth . . . . Feel that energy moving through you, 'grounding' you . . . . Once
you are grounded, you are free to soar to any
heights you wish, and there is never anything
to fear or reject . . . .*

*The pillar has an opening at the top,
too . . . . It opens into the Universe — it is our
connection with the Cosmos . . . .*

*There is a high, shimmering, electric
energy which we can definitely feel, and
which we can, at will, run through our spines
and back out the top . . . .*

*Tune into it . . . gently . . . it is a warm,
shimmering light energy at the top of your
skull . . . your 'Crown Chakra' . . . your connection with infinite intelligence . . . .*

*We are a microcosm — one with the Mac-
rocosm.*

*We are children of earth and children of
light.*

*Feel a healing energy flowing through
your body . . . .*

As you breathe in, feel the energy from the Earth rise up the open pillar of your spine . . . feel it rise right up through the top, uniting with the energy of the Universe . . . .

As you breathe out, feel it shower over the top of you, an exquisite golden etheric Fountain of Life . . . feel it flow down through you, and into the Earth once again . . . cleansing, filling you with light, dissolving all obstacles . . . .

Repeat the breath, several times, imagining, as you breathe in, a vital, healing, glowing, subtle spiritual energy rising up the beautiful tube of your spine, all the way up through the top of your head . . . .

Imagine, as you breathe out, this energy showering down over your whole body, in a fountain of light . . . .

And, as you breathe in, the light collects beneath you and rises through you again . . . and, as you breathe out, it showers over you again, in a pyramid of golden, healing light.

This light is a blessing for you, from your highest self.

Relax . . . enjoy it . . . bask in it. It heals and clarifies your whole being. And you can send this light energy to anyone you wish, anyone who needs a healing or a blessing, with the power of your imagination. Simply raise your hands, palms out, and visualize sending someone the healing energy which is flowing through you. See them bathed in it . . . feel them healed by it . . . see them in perfect health.

> *Take a breath as you finish your medita-*
> *tion. Enjoy the peace and pleasure of your re-*
> *laxed body.*
>   *Your body is a pillar of light.*

Opening up your energy centers

Meditation is quite simple — as you can see if you've tried some of these exercises. One of the most difficult things about meditation is that it is so simple. Most people tend to think it should be more difficult or involve more effort . . . and so they don't think they are doing it correctly, and they quit doing it.

Active meditation involves a very subtle energy, directed by the imagination. Don't work at it too hard — play with it and have fun with it.

Here's another meditation, based on a simple truth which many people don't realize. It if was understood by more people, it would have a great effect in the world, because it is a direct path to personal freedom.

We have the power within us — in our mind, our imagination — to open up every energy center in our body. Our bodies have many different energy centers (*chakra* is the Sanskrit term), and in most people, one or more is blocked somewhat, so that energy isn't really moving freely through the whole being. Most people tend to focus their energy in one or two centers, simply out of habit and earlier conditioning.

In the traditional teachings of India, there are seven major chakras, and several minor ones. In the traditional teachings of the West (such as the Kabbala), five major energy centers are described. It doesn't matter specifically how you choose to break them down. I feel the Western and the Eastern teachings are essentially the same, at their roots.

Each *chakra* is a physical and emotional center of energy; each one corresponds to a major hormonal gland in the body. It is very worthwhile to take the time to explore every one of them — there's a good chance that there are a few you've been ignoring, or a few in which you've been holding a lot of tension, which can sometimes lead to physical and emotional problems if the tension isn't released.

Try this meditation:

> *Sit comfortably, preferably with your spine straight. Or lie horizontally, if you prefer. Get comfortable, and relax . . . .*
>
> *Imagine that there is a light above your head, touching the top of your head — a radiant, glowing ball of spiritual light energy. Imagine that this light is relaxing, soothing, healing the entire area at the top of your skull . . . . Imagine the whole area opening up, releasing and relaxing . . . . Breathe several times, deeply, into this area . . . . Feel the breaths opening, cleansing, releasing, allowing the energy to circulate freely.*
>
> *Now feel the light moving down, into the center of your brain . . . . With your eyes closed, look at the bright light between your brows, in your 'third eye' . . . . Imagine a radiant, glowing ball of spiritual energy is filling your entire head, radiating outward . . . . Imagine that this light is relaxing, soothing, healing the entire area . . . . Breathe several times, deeply, into your head . . . . Feel the breaths opening, cleansing, releasing, allowing the energy to circulate freely.*

Now feel the light moving down again, and centering in your throat.... Imagine a radiant, glowing ball of spiritual energy radiating outward.... Imagine that this light is relaxing, soothing, healing the entire area of your throat.... Breathe several times, deeply, into this area.... Feel the breaths opening, cleansing, releasing, allowing the energy to circulate freely....

Now feel the light moving down again, and centering in your heart.... Imagine a radiant, glowing ball of spiritual energy radiating outward from your heart.... Imagine that this light is relaxing, soothing, healing the entire area of your heart, including your lungs.... Breathe several times, deeply, into this area.... Feel the breaths opening, cleansing, releasing, allowing the energy to circulate freely.... Open up your heart!

Now feel the light moving down again, and centering in your solar plexus and stomach area.... Imagine a radiant, glowing ball of spiritual energy radiating outward from your solar plexus and stomach area.... Imagine that this light is relaxing, soothing, healing the entire area of your solar plexus and stomach, including all internal organs in the area.... Breathe several times, deeply, into this area.... Feel the breaths opening, cleansing, releasing, allowing the energy to circulate freely....

Now feel the light moving down again, and centering in your sexual organs.... Imagine a radiant, glowing ball of spiritual

*energy radiating throughout your whole sex-
ual area.... Imagine that this light is relaxing, soothing, healing the entire area....
Breathe several times, deeply, into this
area.... Feel the breaths opening, cleansing,
releasing, allowing the energy to circulate
freely....*

*Now feel the light moving down again,
and centering at the very base of your spine (if
you are sitting), or in your feet (if you are lying
down). Imagine a radiant, glowing ball of
spiritual energy radiating through the whole
area.... Imagine that this light is relaxing,
soothing, healing the entire area.... Feel the
breaths opening, cleansing, releasing, allowing the energy to circulate freely....*

*Now feel the light radiating, flowing
through all of your energy centers.... Feel the
power of the light.... Become aware that
that light can charge any of your centers which
have become depleted, or blocked.... You are
taking time now to recharge your energy centers....*

*See if you feel any tension in any area. If
you do, send the light to it, and breathe into it.
You can affirm, if you wish, "I am releasing...
I am relaxing... I am letting go of all tension,
all obstacles...."*

*Focus the light in any area you wish....
Breathe into it, for as long as you wish....
Open up all your energy centers!*

Once you begin to experience these energy centers
in your body, you can learn to direct the energy any way

you wish. You are no longer at the mercy of any forces beyond you, whether you feel they're outside forces or internal forces. You are the master of your being — you can choose where to focus your energies. You can direct the course of your destiny, consciously. You are already doing it unconsciously, so you might as well do it consciously.

Creative meditations

Now you're certainly ready to do any number of creative meditations. The effectiveness of creative meditation demonstrates the fact that any image or belief which we hold in our subconscious mind will manifest for us in the world. If we repeatedly tell ourselves that we're going to get cavities from eating white sugar, for instance, we'll get cavities. If we tell ourselves that we can't do something, we won't be able to do it. And if we tell ourselves that we are going to be successful in accomplishing our dreams, we will be successful.

Our bodies and our lives are the results of the conditioning we have accepted on deep, subconscious levels. It is not difficult to affect our subconscious thought processes, and even to change them deeply. All it takes is repeated affirmation, repeated visualization.

If there's something in your life which you would like to change, something you're discontent with, try a creative meditation similar to what follows. Try it for three weeks before giving up on it — and chances are you'll be very satisfied with the results. What you are asking for may require some focused action in the world in addition to your meditation — very few people have made fortunes, for example, by sitting quietly and visualizing it and doing nothing else. But, by doing this kind of creative meditation, you will receive guidance from your own intuitive master — guidance which will tell you exactly what is necessary to do to achieve that which you desire.

Do the following meditation — and then stay open to the ideas, impulses, 'hunches' which come to you as a result of it.

Get comfortable... relax.... Take a deep breath, and as you exhale, affirm, "My body is now relaxing." Take another deep breath, and as you exhale, affirm, "My mind is now relaxed." Take one more deep breath, and as you exhale, affirm, "I am letting everything go."

Then, clearly visualize, imagine, exactly that which you want to create for yourself.... See and feel yourself doing it, being it, having it as clearly as you can, in as detailed a manner as you can. Feel yourself expanding to be able to do it, be it, or have it. Feel all obstacles falling away.

Make up affirmations which tell your subconscious mind that you deserve it, and that you have it, here and now. Take a moment to enjoy having it. Give thanks for it.

Finish by saying to yourself, "This, or something better, is now manifesting for the highest good of all concerned, in totally satisfying and harmonious ways. So be it. So it is."

Do this meditation often enough so that you carry it with you throughout your day. Keep putting your energy into it. Perhaps at first you will simply *feel* a change, without experiencing anything in the outer world. Then you may get an idea, think of something to do, someone to contact, whatever. And soon, with repeated visualization — repeated long enough for your subconscious to get it deeply, and prepare for it — the door of opportunity will open for you, and you will achieve whatever your heart has desired.

I am not the first to be saying these words, by any means. Many, many teachers and writers, from all over the world, have been saying it for centuries: *"Ask, and you shall receive."*

A meditation on our three bodies

Here is a meditation which contains many deep truths — if you have ears to hear, and eyes to see . . . .

Many traditions, from both the East and the West — such as Buddhism and the Kabbala — teach that we have *three* bodies, not just one, as it appears to us on a purely physical level. The following has many correspondences to the description of the process of creation (in Chapter III.)

Our first body is the physical body — the body we can see, feel, and touch with our five outer, physical senses. It is the physical plane (called the *nirmana kaya* in Tibetan Buddhism):

> *Sit and relax and tune into your physical body. . . . Observe your breathing, your heartbeat. . . . Notice how it takes effortless care of itself, ever healing, ever renewing. There is nothing to reject about our physical bodies. They are a miracle of creation.*

Our second body is a very light, shimmering body
— a body created by our thoughts and feelings, whether
consciously or unconsciously. It is often called the astral body in Western traditions (and the *sambhoga kaya*
in Buddhism):

> *Sit and relax and tune into your astral
> body . . . . The astral body is the body we
> create with the finer, inner senses of the im-
> agination and inner vision and other inner
> intuitive senses, such as our feelings . . . . It is
> the body we can create for ourselves in our
> mind's inner eye — it is what enables us to
> create anything we wish, in our im-
> agination . . . .*
>
> *It is on this plane of imagination and
> inner vision where magic happens . . . where
> the things we wish to create take form . . . . It
> is the astral plane which is the plane on which
> creation takes place — before anything is
> manifest on the physical plane, it must first be
> imagined on the astral plane . . . .*
>
> *Play with your astral body, like a child.
> Travel anywhere in your imagination. Create
> any kind of life for yourself which you want.
> Give yourself total freedom.*
>
> *Imagine yourself as radiantly healthy,
> strong, beautiful. Imagine yourself doing
> exactly what you dream of doing. Create in
> your mind, with a relaxed body, anything your
> heart desires . . . .*

Notice how you feel as you finish your astral journey. The astral plane is much more than 'pure imagina-

tion' which has no effect on the physical world. It is *creative* imagination, for it literally creates the forms on a subtle plane which will, in time, if we're persistent, become manifest on the physical plane.

You don't even have to worry *how* the things which you are creating on the astral plane are going to manifest. Just keep picturing the thing you want, keep the end result in mind. Soon the means to achieve that end will come to you — perhaps in a dream, or upon awakening, or in a moment of insight, or in a daydream. Then the steps will become clear to you. Accomplishing anything is just one simple step after another: a phone call, an appointment, writing a page, creating a brochure, etc. Keep visualizing your goal, and trust your intuition to lead you to that goal.

Our third body is the highest and most magnificent body of all: it is the body which encompasses all, the body which links us with the entire universe, the all-embracing body, 'beyond words' (called the *dharma kaya* — 'body of truth' — in Tibetan Buddhism).

> *Sit and relax deeply.... Let everything go... be silent.... Tune into the wholeness of you, which is a part of, and no different from, the rest of the universe.... Focus on your highest spiritual nature.... It is the source of creation....*
>
> *Pick any of the following words which are particularly resonant with you, and sit with them, in silence:*
> *I am the Ultimate Truth, beyond all relative truths, beyond all words...*
> *I am Absolute Reality...*
> *I am Christ Consciousness...*

I am Buddha Nature...
I am shimmering emptiness... the crea-
tive void... the ever-empty yet full
seed of creation...
I am what is...
I am part of the atomic unity of every
created thing...
I am the beyond...
I am the Source...
I am Eternity...
I am the Kingdom of Heaven...
I am my own true being...
I am my highest self...
I am pure bliss...
I am Oneness...

Take your time coming out of this deep meditation. Take some time to just sit in silence, savoring and nurturing all three of your wondrous bodies.

Be with yourself

In case we lost you on that last exercise, we'll come back to something very simple — child's play, in fact. A very effective form of creative meditation is to just open yourself up to the ideas, fantasies, impulses that come to you naturally when you're alone — whether you're walking, sitting, playing, even doing many types of work....

Take some time to be with yourself. Take some time to just sit there and do nothing....

There's a story about Abraham Lincoln that I heard when I was a child, and never forgot:

At one time, when Abe and his brothers were

teenagers, they were all supposed to be splitting rails for a fence around their land. But Abe kept wandering out into the woods, and sitting there doing nothing, lost in his thoughts.

Finally, Abe's brothers went to his father and complained, saying that Abe wasn't getting any of the work done. Abe's father must have been a wise man, because he said to his sons, "Just let him be... sometimes a person needs time to think."

Take time for yourself, every once in a while, to just slow down and relax. Sit with a plant, a tree.... Lie on your back, and stare up at the clouds, like you used to do when you were young....

Watch a river flow... watch a flower grow... and you watch your life flow... and you see yourself grow... and you see Life... and you awaken your intuitive understanding....

> *Look up into a clear night's sky*
> *When you can see for*
> *a billion light years*

> *Then you can see*
> *Infinity*
> *beyond our smiles and tears*

Closing the gates

Here's an exercise which can have a deep effect, if you let it. It's called 'Closing the gates':

Sit comfortably, with your spine straight.
Take a moment to relax. Close your eyes, and
take several deep breaths, rhythmically, relax-

*ing more with every breath. Then raise your
hands to your face, palms facing you.*

*Place your left thumb over your left ear
and your right thumb over your right ear, shut-
ting off the sound as effectively and as comfortably as possible. Place your forefingers
over your eyelids, blocking out external light
as effectively and comfortably as possible.
Then, take a deep breath, and block your nostrils with your next finger. Then, place your
ring finger and little finger over your mouth.*

*You have now 'closed the gates'. Sit in
silence and observe. When you need to
breathe, let go of the fingers blocking your
nostrils, and breathe comfortably as you keep
closing the gates with your other fingers.*

Usually, I don't try to describe the results of an
exercise too specifically, because everyone's experience
is different. But in this exercise, I had a remarkable
experience, which I attempted to put into words in an
earlier book, *Chrysalis*: "The effect was wondrous. I
was plunged into a vast 'inner space' — as vast as oceans.
Suddenly, there were whole new worlds to explore . . .
worlds I had dreamed of when I was a kid, but had
forgotten . . . worlds of magic . . . worlds of the mind,
created in an instant by the mind."

Mantra

Sit quietly and comfortably for a moment. Pick a
phrase, or *mantra*, or affirmation, to focus on and to
repeat. Repeat it with feeling, until you *experience* it.

A *mantra* is a chant, a repeated spoken word or

series of words. Some mantras are simple, some are complex; some are in Sanskrit, some in English or other languages. Pick any that feel good to you. Some examples are:

Om Mani Padme Hum

(or in English):

> *Hail to the jewel of bliss*
> *In the lotus of consciousness!*

> *We know who we are, we are one*

> *Sri Ram, Jai Ram, Jai Jai Rama*

> *OM*

> *Be in peace*

> *The kingdom of heaven is within*

> *Om namo Shivaya*

> *May the long time sun shine upon us*
>   *All love surround us*
> *And the pure light within us*
>   *Guide our way home*

> *I am free ... I am strong*

> *The light of God surrounds us*
>   *The love of God unfolds us*
> *The power of God flows through us*
>   *Wherever I am, God is, and all is well.*

The last chant, above, is a prayer of protection, especially suitable for any times you happen to feel fearful or vulnerable.

Yoga and tantra

This entire book is actually about *yoga* — yoga for the West. There have been many, many books on yoga — but then, it is a vast subject, and it is continually evolving.

There are some teachers of tantra in the Eastern tradition who separate it from yoga, saying there is the path of yoga and the path of tantra, and the two are directly opposite. But this is not true in my understanding or experience. Tantra is a form of yoga, tantra is a way of life which encompasses every form of yoga — tantra is the yoga of every moment of your life. The practice of tantra is the yoga of those who are ready for a much broader definition of both yoga and tantra than may be currently popular.

Yoga in its broadest and deepest root-word sense means 'union', which is the same root-word meaning as 'religion', which means 're-uniting'. The practice of yoga leads ultimately to a deep realization of your union with the Universe, union with your highest self and highest purpose. The root-word of tantra means 'to weave' — for *tantra* is the stuff of life, the fabric of our entire life, the experience of every moment.

The highest levels of awareness can use both 'yoga' and 'tantra' together — for the two are not mutually exclusive. 'Tantra yoga' is a rapid and powerful path: it is *the awareness which leads to finding our highest expression within every moment of daily life, rejecting nothing.* Every moment we are studying tantra. And every moment we are doing yoga, in the broadest sense of the word.

Still, it is very useful and healthful at times to do specific yoga practices. I'll describe a few forms which have been particularly good for me — both traditional and non-traditional.

Hatha yoga

Hatha yoga is the traditional series of physical exercises which most people associate with the word 'yoga'. Many teachers also include *pranayama,* or breathing exercises, and meditation along with the study of hatha yoga. There are many fine teachers of hatha yoga around, in nearly every major city. And there are many excellent books and tapes on the subject.

The best hatha yoga exercises are non-strenuous, and very good for body and mind. One of the best cassette tapes of yoga instruction I know of is "Yoga with Chi-uh" (available through the publishers of this book). I recommend hatha yoga very highly. It has an immediate effect: strengthening, healing, and calming. But don't beat yourself up if you miss your yoga session.

Kum Nye

There is a very effective form of physical yoga which the Tibetans teach, called *kum nye,* or 'body relaxation'. Now many different forms of therapy and healing in the West incorporate similar kinds of physical exercises.

You can do it yourself, unassisted, or you can do it with others.

> *Simply relax for a moment ... take a few deep breaths ... and start poking, probing, and rubbing your body (or your friend's body) .... You can, if you wish, start at the head and neck, and work down. Or start with any high tension area.*
>
> *Explore your body, gently, yet firmly .... Search for tensions — especially in your stomach area, under your ribs, in your neck and shoulders, and chest .... When you find a tense spot, tune into it and massage it deeply ... send it a warm, deep, loving, healing vibration ... imagine it dissolving, releasing ... breathe deeply into it, and feel it release .... Do whatever you need to do physically to release it ... you may want to make sounds, or move in a certain way .... Let your breath, sound, and movement dissolve that tension .... Just visualize it dissolving, and let it go.*
>
> *Finish by just relaxing and breathing quietly.*

Sometimes — especially in your neck and shoulder area, and in your feet, and along the bones of your lower legs — you can actually feel the tension in the form of a small lump or 'crystal'. It may actually be crystalized energy which is blocked. By rubbing deeply into these crystals, and imagining them releasing as you exhale deeply, you can sometimes actually feel them dissolving, and feel a release, a lightening up of the tension you are carrying with you.

One nice touch is to rub the earlobes from top to bottom in a stroking manner, between your thumb and forefinger. It is very relaxing; it's even good for getting kids to sleep.

Do this whole exercise, and you *will* release your tension, for it is in our power to dissolve all unnecessary tension in our bodies. For our tension, too, is empty, like everything else. It too is pure energy, pure light, like everything else . . . .

Free form yoga

This exercise — a form of 'non-traditional yoga' — can take just a very short time. It is simple, and it is healing, physically and emotionally. Give it a try.

> *Stand up (or lie down if you feel like it) and focus your attention on your feelings . . . get out of your head and into your gut feelings. Take a breath or two, and move deeply into your feelings . . . . Start to breathe, to move, slowly or rapidly, depending on what you're feeling.*
>
> *Just follow your feelings . . . . Don't* think *about what you're doing at all. As soon as you find yourself thinking about it, drop down into your feelings again, and just* move *in any way that feels good.*
>
> *Absolutely any type of movement — including stillness — is allowed, and encouraged . . . . Do whatever you have the energy to do.*

Do it for a minute or two, or for an hour — as long as it lasts. Use it to release, to relax, to take a break, to stretch your body . . . to yawn, to lie still, to dance . . .

to jump, to fly, to slowly stretch ... maybe to yell or shout, or shake your body vigorously ... to do exercises, to do yoga, to do whatever your body wants to do ....

Give yourself the time to do this exercise. It's a very effective form of meditation and yoga. It gets you into your feelings and out of your head ... into your intuitive body/mind and out of your rational mind .... And it exercises, heals, releases tensions, and opens you up to receiving much more energy from the ever-abundant Universe.

The Way is Infinite

There is a season for everything ....

A time for discipline ... a time to let discipline go.

A time to read, a time not to read.

A time to go to workshops, meditations, group gatherings ... and a time not to go.

A time to have a teacher ... and a time to be your own master.

A time to question, and a time not to question ....

A time of faith ... a time of skepticism ....

A time to get into some kind of growth-oriented or spiritual or artistic or scientific or business activity, and a time to get out of it ....

The Way is Infinite .... Everyone has their own path — endless variations on the same theme, endlessly growing in wisdom and compassion, endlessly growing toward freedom and perfection.

We have the power to rebuild ourselves anew, if we but awaken to the power of our inner creative visualizations.

XII

Aging and Healing

We live in a culture which extols the virtues of youth and which has forgotten the value of old age. Being young and vital is a beautiful thing, and it deserves to be celebrated and enjoyed. And yet, as people start to age, there is no need to reject it in any way. Aging is part of a great natural process, and every step of that process has its own beauty and perfection.

A youthful observation

When I was in my mid-teens, my father was approaching fifty. One day, two friends of his came by to visit. They had all gone to high school together, and they were the same biological age. But as I looked at the three of them together, I was astounded by something — and I knew that in some way it was very significant, but I didn't know why at the time. Only years later did it make any sense.

One of my father's friends looked like a very old man, close to seventy, bald, short-winded, slow and stiff. And the other looked like a very young man, about thirty, healthy, strong, filled with youthful energy. My father looked about his age — somewhere between the two.

I remember asking myself, repeatedly, why these two men of the same age looked to be such different ages. One could have been the other's father! It didn't make sense to me at the time — because I was assuming that aging was a process which somehow occurs at the same rate for all people. But obviously, these two men were aging at different rates. One was old, one was young. Several months later, my father told me that the old looking one had died. I wasn't surprised at all. That was close to 20 years ago. The young looking man, now in his 60s, still looks young, and still works full time, active, creative, and healthy.

The aging process

There are several things which affect our aging process, and which are directly related to our physical, emotional, and mental processes.

On a physical level, our diet and exercise certainly affect the aging process. I am not a pure foods fanatic by any means, but I do see that if a person abuses their body with too much food, too much alcohol, not enough exercise, then their body is naturally going to start slowing down and developing problems.

Our emotional and mental processes seem to affect our aging even more than the physical, for we are constantly giving our bodies operating instructions with our minds and our feelings. These instructions are often on 'subconscious' levels. In reality, there is nothing in our minds or feelings that is actually 'subconscious', for all we need to do is to focus the light of our inner observation upon what we're feeling and what we're telling ourselves, and the so-called subconscious patterns emerge. If we're telling ourselves, on deep levels, that we're young and strong and healthy, we're going to stay young and strong and healthy. If we're telling ourselves that we're weak, or prone to sickness, or fat, or whatever, we're going to continue to create that for ourselves.

Think yourself thin

Many people have difficulty seeing how this process works. Let's take an overweight person as an example. Imagine that you are five feet, five inches tall and weigh 300 pounds. You've put so much fat on your body that you have difficulty moving. Why are you so fat? Many people believe it's because of hormonal imbalance, which is true — but the imbalance is an *effect* of something deeper, and not the root cause.

A large part of that root cause is the amount of food you are putting into your body: you are taking in more than you're fully processing. But yet, there are a great many fat people who eat less than thin people. Why is this? Many people say it's their metabolism — some people are blessed with an active metabolism which totally digests and some are unfortunate enough to have a slow metabolism, which surrounds them in fat. There is a degree of truth in this, but again it is not the root cause of your fat condition. Why is your metabolism sluggish while others are more active?

Certainly your level of physical activity affects

your metabolism. One good way to lose weight is to get more exercise. But there is something else which is an even deeper root cause of fat: *it is what you're telling yourself*, repeatedly on deep levels, which is determining how much weight you're holding onto. If you are constantly telling yourself, "I'm fat," or "This food is making me fat," your body will follow these instructions and create exactly the fat body which you are fearing, yet drawing to yourself.

If, on the other hand, you start telling yourself, repeatedly in the mornings and throughout the day, that you are thin and healthy, your body will start responding to these instructions, and the weight will start coming off.

Say you weigh 300 or 400 pounds. Obviously, you've been telling yourself you are fat. If you start telling yourself you are thin, no matter how ridiculous it may seem to you, no matter how irrational, you are going to create some changes for yourself. The first changes will be subtle. Now that you're telling yourself that you are thin (even though you aren't!), your posture is going to improve. You will start carrying all your weight more easily, and you will feel lighter, even though you're still breaking the bathroom scale. If you stay with the affirmation, "I am thin, I am beautiful" throughout the day, for several weeks, especially every time you catch yourself telling yourself otherwise, your body will gradually conform to your consistent thought form, as it always does. It may take some time, but gradually, you will think yourself thin. Or beautiful. Or younger. Or whatever your heart desires.

Why not? You deserve it! It's certainly worth a try ... and easier than many diets.

If these affirmations don't work for you, you may

have some deep emotional reasons for wanting or need-
ing to be fat which will have to be examined and dealt
with. For example, some people hold onto excess weight
as a psychic protection or out of a desire to punish
themselves or from fear of being too beautiful, desirable,
or powerful. Usually, as you deal more with your deep
feelings and learn to express them, the weight starts
dissolving as your emotional blocks dissolve.

An exercise

*Take a clear, objective look at your body,
right at this moment. Is it fat? thin? strong?
weak? beautiful? ugly? old? young? lethargic?
active? sagging? firm?*

*Describe your body to yourself. Then
realize that your body is the concrete physical
result of years of emotional and mental conditioning which you have been giving yourself... or which you have accepted without
questioning or denying from someone else.*

*Make up some affirmations which men-
tally and emotionally create the type of body
you want. Give yourself these affirmations,
with force and certainty — even if your mind
is saying they're ridiculous and false.*

*Whenever you run into this inner resis-
tance, overcome it with another positive affirmation.*

These kinds of affirmations are sometimes difficult
for people to accept, because it seems as if you are
blatantly lying to yourself. In a way, that's true — but
you are lying for a good cause, and it will have a good

effect. In order for us to create anything, we must first imagine it mentally and feel it emotionally, creating an inner *experience* of the reality we want to create next. Our affirmations are creating the blueprints for our future evolution.

Create a young beautiful body

I once knew a woman who was well into middle age, but had the looks and the skin tone of a teenager. I asked her what her secret was, and she said, "It's in the family. My mother has great skin tone, so does my sister." Because she had been affirming that all her life, instead of worrying about losing her tone (and thereby putting energy into creating just what she was afraid of), she had created a young, beautiful body.

There are techniques for creating a healthy, beautiful body. Simple affirmations alone will do it — make up your own. Or here are other techniques — first a short version, then a longer version:

> *Short version:*
> *Sit, or lie down, in a comfortable position. Take a few breaths, and relax your body, your mind, and your entire being . . . . Then simply imagine a body of light enveloping you — imagine your ideal body, strong and young and beautiful, however you wish to see it . . . imagine that you are drawing that body to you, and that you are merging with it, and becoming it. Imagine your physical body conforming to your newly created light body, so that your physical body is actually changing, growing stronger and more beautiful.*

Focus the light of your mind's eye in any particular area of your body where you want special change, special attention. Create the body you wish in your mind's eye, and know that you are on your way to creating it physically.

Find an affirmation or two to complete the exercise. Perhaps, "I am young and strong" or "My body is growing younger, stronger, and more beautiful every day."

Get up, and stretch, and feel younger and stronger and healthier and more beautiful.

Longer version:

Begin with the exercise described on page 138 — "Opening up your energy centers." Move light through your entire body, awakening each center of energy within you . . . . Imagine your body to be a glowing, vibrating light body . . . . Imagine that it is elastic and changeable.

'Run energy' through your whole body, directed by your mind's eye. Begin with your feet, and imagine energy moving up your left side to the top of your head, then down your right side to your feet, then up again . . . . Do this a few times . . . . Then run the energy from your feet up your back to the top of your head, then down the front of your body and back to your feet again . . . . Do this a few times, too, imagining that the light energy is cleansing, refreshing, rebuilding your entire body . . . .

Then run energy from your feet straight up your spine, all the way to the top of your

*head.... Let it shower over your whole body,
bathing you in a fountain of golden light
energy.... Then gather it up at your feet
again and bring it up your spine again.... Do
this a few times, imagining that you are
bathing yourself in the elixir of life, the fountain of youth....*

*Now you've awakened your whole
physical/emotional/mental/spiritual system
with the power of your energy directed by your
mind. Now you can direct this energy to any
part of your body you wish, healing, rejuvenating, rebuilding your body as you wish. Feel the
energy building new muscle, tightening your
skin tone, dissolving tension.... Feel the
energy creating exactly the type of body you
wish.*

Create a young, beautiful body in your mind's eye.
Your physical form will soon follow.

In the meantime, however, don't reject your current physical condition. Love and appreciate the body
you have, the gifts you have been given. There is a
perfection in every one, at every moment: this is the
teaching of tantra.

A face exercise

The above exercises can be used specifically on
your face. Using them, you can create a face which is
more relaxed, more beautiful, more vital, filled with
light.

Simply relax, close your eyes.... Feel the

energy in your body . . . feel it in your face . . . .
Now use that energy to give yourself a facial —
you can do it physically, with your hands, you
can have a friend do it to you, or you can
simply do it mentally, with your mind's
eye . . . . The way you do it doesn't matter. Just
be sure to visualize tension dissolving . . . vis-
ualize wrinkles dissolving, fading away . . .
visualize your features becoming more
beautiful . . . visualize light energy in your
eyes . . . visualize youthful fullness and
color . . . . Visualize your ideal face . . . create
it . . . enjoy it . . . love it!

If you do this exercise repeatedly, you will begin to
notice changes — first very subtle ones, then very obvious ones. We have the power to rebuild ourselves anew,
if we but awaken to the power of our repeated inner
creative visualizations.

The principles of healing

Healing can occur on any of our four levels of being.
Healing is an entirely organic, natural process. Our
bodies are healing themselves all the time, cleansing,
purifying, strengthening. Our bodies are designed to
function easily, effortlessly, and without pain. Pain is
simply a message to ourselves that something needs to
be changed.

There are no 'incurable' diseases. Our bodies are
always curing themselves, if we aren't blocking the cure
and if we aren't actually desiring the sickness on some
deep level because there's a payoff in it for us — sym-
pathy, attention, love, getting out of an uncomfortable

situation, or whatever. Your body was designed to be perfectly healthy. If it isn't, focus on one or more of the following levels:

> *Physical level:*
> *Take time to relax your body, and let the body's natural healing processes occur, with as little interference from you as possible. If the 'affected' part of your body is too cool, warm it up; if it is too warm, cool it off; if it is too dry, keep it moist; if it is too wet, keep it dry. But basically, just relax, eat very simple, pure foods, and give your body time to heal itself.*

> *Emotional level:*
> *Don't resist being sick — accept it. Your body needs to rest, so give it time to relax. Accept all your feelings . . . express them to a sympathetic friend.*
> *Ask yourself honestly, and repeatedly if necessary, what you are feeling emotionally that is causing this disease? Have you been feeling resentful? Have you been feeling burned out at work and in need of a break? Have you been feeling that you can't express yourself to others? Often, just giving yourself permission to fully express your feelings can dissolve sickness at the root.*

> *Mental level:*
> *What do you truly think is the cause of your illness or disease? A deep part of you knows the answer. What is the root cause,*

beneath the symptoms? It's all in your mind. Picture yourself strong, and well.

Spiritual level:
There is no disease. You are a perfect be-ing. Arise and walk and be strong and healthy. Your faith has made you whole.

Keep growing

There's no need to grow *old* — simply grow, and keep growing.... We are designed by nature to keep expanding our horizons, endlessly, becoming stronger, clearer, more aware and more powerful with each pass-ing year. Affirm this to be, and it will be!

We have power, if we just embrace that power.

XIII

Politics

The last few decades have witnessed a great change in the mass mind of America. A deeper level of awareness has emerged, which is finding new ways to live in the world, and new ways to relate to each other. This awakening comes at a very necessary time, for the current thinking which is still dominating governments, politics, and business has created huge dinosaurs which are rapidly becoming extinct.

The culture as a whole, led by its most progressive thinkers and doers, is rediscovering its own intuitive nature, which has been stifled, almost obliterated, by the rational, 'scientific' takeover of the Western culture over the last several centuries. We are learning to again balance the rational with the intuitive. We are learning to create a science and a politics which doesn't reject the intuitive, the emotional, the sensitive, the spiritual.

As this intuitive awareness began to again come to the surface of the mass consciousness, there seemed to be a huge schism between the intuitive and the rational, between the 'spiritual' and the 'political' or 'scientific'. The infant intuitive force couldn't survive along with the fierce, intense energies of the political and scientific, and so had to divorce itself from them, and nurture itself in private.

This intuitive awareness has now gained sufficient strength to deal with any and all forces which shape our lives and our destinies, and so this new age which is dawning is beginning to see a unique blending of the intuitive and the scientific, and of the spiritual and political. Actually, it isn't unique: Mahatma Gandhi successfully blended both the spiritual and political many years ago — and Gandhi was in turn influenced by Emerson and Thoreau, highly progressive American writers.

The schism is over. We no longer have to separate the spiritual and political. We no longer have to avoid certain areas of activity in order to protect our new awareness. The whole world is our playground and laboratory for the great experiment of our lives. And we can play in any and every arena of life that we wish.

Your personal power

As creative, free individuals, we have a great deal of personal power, to be exercised both spiritually and politically, to be exercised everywhere. The last few decades have proven to us that individuals do have a great deal of power politically, once they find skillful means to express that power.

Daniel Ellsberg recently said on national television that Nixon, when he was President, had a plan — appropriately called the 'madman project' — to end the

Vietnam War in the same way the Korean War was ended: through threat of a nuclear attack which would be far more devastating than Hiroshima. The North Vietnamese were offered an ultimatum, backed up with nuclear power. But, unlike North Korea, North Vietnam didn't accept the ultimatum. And, according to Ellsberg's reporting, Nixon was fully prepared to put the 'madman project' into effect and get us into an atomic war. Fortunately, this coincided with a huge series of demonstrations against the war, where hundreds of thousands of people marched in Washington D.C. and San Francisco and other cities. Nixon realized that he didn't have the support of the American people, and he didn't dare put his well-named plan into effect.

In effect, it was the American people — those who organized and marched, and those who spoke out in other ways — who avoided nuclear war. We have power, if we but embrace that power. There are many, many different creative channels through which we can express that power. But we have to make some major changes if we're to live in an environment that's worth living in.

The deep meaning of karma

There is a word which is at the core of the great wisdom which many Eastern countries are now offering the West: the word is the Sanskrit word *karma*, and it is a concept which the West is only now beginning to understand. And we must understand it, and practice it, if we are going to continue to grow and be healthy, and not decay and crumble . . . .

The law of karma is the law of cause and effect: *for every action we put into the world, we receive an equal and appropriate reaction.* The law of karma explains why a thief will get ripped off, why an angry person lives in an angry world, and why a loving person lives in a loving world.... We reap what we sow.

Karma operates in our lives individually, and it operates for the whole human race on this planet. The West has created a great many difficulties for the whole world by being completely unconscious of the law of karma, even though this law was the essence of the teachings of the West's most enlightened master:

> *"Love one another"... "Do unto others as you would have them do unto you"... "As you sow, so shall you reap."*

The white race in particular has made some grave karmic mistakes in the way we have dealt with every other race on the globe. No wonder we have bred frustration and anger around the world. We all must change some basic attitudes. We must *all* — every race, every group — ask for personal, clear guidance, for the understanding which will show us the skillful means by which we may overcome our past mistakes, collectively and individually.

We all must learn to forgive, and accept others.

We all must stop fighting others.

We must stop living at other people's expense.

We must take responsibility for the abolition, within our lifetimes, of racism, starvation, poverty, and exploitation in our global community. It can be done, if we turn our powers of creative visualization upon these issues.

We must remember the teachings of the greatest master who has influenced the West, who understood karma completely, and taught it, and lived it.

We've got to start now, making these changes on an inner, individual level. Soon more and more outer forms will emerge to facilitate these changes. Some have emerged already, such as the many environmental protection groups like Greenpeace and Friends of the Earth, the anti-nuclear movement, the Hunger Project, and countless others. There are many things we can do, as individuals and collectively. Our own inner guidance can best lead us.

We live in exciting times, times of change and growth. Some people are embracing the changes enthusiastically. Some, like dinosaurs, will resist the signs of necessary change until they fall and perish for lack of adaptability. It all depends on your karma — on the things you have done, and the things you do today and tomorrow.

New Age politics

None of us live in a vacuum. Everything we do affects others. It is time to create a politics which fully appreciates and balances the interests of all people. 'Old age politics' and other old age business practices are on their way out — dying from their own lack of vision and adaptability. By 'old age' politics and business, I mean those forms of activity which create situations where some people take unfair advantage of other people, where some are fattened to an extreme and others are deprived, where there is a 'win-lose' relationship. At its extreme, old age politics and business could lead to nuclear war — a total 'lose-lose' proposition, fueled by insanity.

'New age' politics and business creates 'win-win'

relationships which support everyone involved. There is no need for anyone to take advantage of anyone else. There is plenty for all, if we but see it, and create it. We can all live in abundance — every person on this planet — if we quit taking advantage of each other, and work and live in harmony.

It can be done. It is already being done, in many forms. It is up to each of us to create more of these forms, and to expand the present forms until their impact is felt in the mass consciousness, and until we transform our world into a beautiful and supportive place for all.

Affirm it to be true, and it is true.

So be it. So it is!

All your limitations, all your shortcomings, are imaginary. You are, in truth, an unlimited being . . . .

All we need to do is to connect with our essence. All we need to do is to see what we really are, and we are enlightened.

XIV

Enlightenment

The word 'enlightenment', like the word 'tantra', is used in so many different ways by so many different people with so many different definitions that it becomes meaningless unless it is clearly defined and understood.

According to most forms of Tibetan Buddhism, enlightenment is the very top of the mountain of our ever-evolving consciousness, the culmination of lifetime after lifetime of searching and discovering — a peak so distant and remote for most people that only one person in each great age, the Buddha, ever achieves real enlightenment.

According to many forms of Zen Buddhism, however, enlightenment is an experience which can come in a moment to anyone who is receptive to it. The "kensho" experience, as it is called, is a deep, even if sometimes momentary, experience of oneness, of bliss, of completeness, which many, many people have had.

Enlightenment is whatever you define it to be. You can believe that you will never achieve it — and you will never achieve it. You can believe that you will achieve it at some time in the future, when you finally get yourself together — and you may or may not create it for yourself in the future, depending on whether you change your belief or not, and finally create it in the present tense. You can believe that you already *are* enlightened — that it is your true, natural, highest state of being — and you are enlightened.

All teachings of the enlightenment experience point within us, and show us that enlightenment is our truest essence. All we need to do is to connect with our essence, to see what really is, and we are enlightened.

A Tibetan teacher told me the following story, a metaphor describing the process and nature of enlightenment:

> *One night, a woman had an intensely vivid dream, so vivid that she thought it was real. She dreamed that she lost her head, literally — she dreamed that her head was missing from her shoulders.*
>
> *The next morning, she woke up and frantically went searching for her head. She searched everywhere for it, and she could not find it. Her desperate cries for it didn't do any good.*
>
> *Finally, she went to a teacher, and asked where she could find her head. The teacher simply held up a mirror for her to see herself. And she realized that she had had it all along, and it was only in a dream that she had lost it.*

This story is a beautiful metaphor for the process and nature of enlightenment. The central character is a woman rather than a man — this symbolizes the intuitive within each of us, the fact that our enlightenment lies within our intuitive nature, the feminine principle within us, rather than within our rational nature, the masculine principle within us. Searching desperately for your own intuitive nature will never reveal it to you. You must simply find someone or something which is a mirror for you — something which will reflect your true, intuitive nature to you. You must simply see that all of your friends, and everything in your living and working environment, is a mirror for you, reflecting your state of mind. Take all of this feedback to heart, without blaming yourself in any way — without judging or criticizing. Just absorb it, and be willing to make any changes that are necessary, any changes that your own intuitive wisdom tells you are appropriate for you.

Look closely at yourself, and you will one day discover that all your limitations, all your shortcomings, are imaginary. You are, in truth, an unlimited being. Your body and mind are literally composed of light energy. You are enlightened, here and now. You always have been, and you always will be. Just see that this is so, and it is so.

There is a deep and wonderful teaching which has been given in many different words, in many different traditions, both Eastern and Western. To put it simply:

> *We are much greater beings than we think we are. We have higher levels of consciousness, and even higher bodies than we perceive. We all have a Christ consciousness, we all have a Buddha nature, within us. Our natural state of being is one of enlightenment.*

You don't have to seek elsewhere for your answers, for your greatest treasures. They are found within you. Affirm to yourself:

> *I am enlightened, here and now.*

And it is so.

You were meant to be as free as a bird, or as a star, or as any master that has walked this earth.

XV

Freedom

To sum it up — a final exercise

At the beginning of this book, we defined tantra as *the awareness that creates complete personal freedom within every moment of daily life, rejecting nothing.* Then we applied this principle of tantra — this open awareness — to many of the most important areas of our lives.

Here is a final practice, to sum it up:

> *Ask yourself, "What is it about _____ that I need to understand?"* .... *In the blank space, insert the titles of the chapters of this book — relationships, sex, being alone, work, money, creativity, aging, politics, etc. — or any other areas of your life which are there for you now to deal with. Look at every answer that surfaces for you.*

> *Then ask yourself, "What is it about my*
> _____ *that is teaching me to*
> *be free?" — inserting the same word in the*
> *blank space.*
> *Repeat the questions, and allow yourself*
> *to absorb whatever answers come up for you.*

For example: Ask yourself, "What is it about my relationships that I need to understand?" Then answer yourself, in whatever words that pop into your mind. Then ask again, then answer again, until you feel satisfied with the answer. Then ask, "What is it about my relationships that is teaching me to be free?" Answer yourself again, until you feel satisfied.

This exercise — simple though it is, for anyone — can tune you into your intuitive teacher. It is usually better to ask yourself questions, rather than asking other people. Who knows you better than yourself?

Shattering models

At some point in our growth process, we have to confront and understand all the 'models' which we have created for ourselves, and which we have accepted from other people. These are emotional and intellectual models of how we *should* be, and *shouldn't* be, what we *should* do, and *shouldn't* do, what we *should* have, and *shouldn't* have. These models are deeply ingrained, from very early conditioning.

There comes a time when we become mature enough — in the highest sense of the word — to go beyond any and all of these models. You can do, be, and have anything you wish, in your heart. Get married, or stay single . . . or get divorced. Have children, or don't have children. Love a woman, or love a man. Love several women, or love several men . . . love a man and a woman, love several men and women . . . . Make a fortune, or make nothing. Be rich, be poor. Be a success, be a failure. Work for a corporation, work for yourself . . . or don't work at all. Be spiritual, or worldly . . . or political, or scientific . . . get into computers, or covens . . . . You are free to do exactly as you wish — exactly as your heart desires.

At some point in our development, the only thing blocking us from true freedom is our own model of what that freedom is. If we are truly free, we are free to do anything, to be anything, to have anything. So let all models go! And you will be free. Shatter all your models. Let the judge in you go. Simply don't allow yourself to judge yourself in any negative way. And you will be free.

Tune into the guidance of your intuition, and give yourself permission to realize your own true nature.

You are free if you affirm yourself to be

One of the deepest — perhaps *the* deepest — teachings we have repeatedly dealt with in this book is that *what you consistently affirm to yourself soon becomes true in your experience.*

Argue for your limitations, and they are yours. But affirm to yourself that you are free — and soon you will find yourself creating a reality in which you are a totally free being, free to do what you wish, to be what you wish, and to have what you wish.

This is your birthright. You were meant to be as free as a bird, or as a star, or as any master that has walked this earth. Embrace your freedom! It is yours for the taking. All you have to do is to affirm to yourself, repeatedly,

I am free!

And you are free . . . free to be whatever you dream of being. This is true. I know it in my heart.

May you be blessed
with whatever
your heart desires

So be it — so it is!

Appendix A

Tantra in the East: A Brief, Unscholarly History of Tibetan Tantric Buddhism

Tibetan Buddhism is the 'tantric' branch of Buddhism. Here is an overview of it, gleaned from several years of study. It is not a scholarly approach — the scholarly approach is being well represented by numerous writers and teachers. This is, instead, a compilation of writings and stories which I have picked up from the Tibetan people themselves, and presented in an informal fashion — in the spirit in which I encountered most of this information.

First, I'll present you with a brief, unscholarly history of *tantra,* then we'll see its meaning and usefulness for the West today. Most of this has been picked up through my study of the *Nyingma* tradition of Tibetan Buddhism, so if it seems to glorify that one, and slightly minimize the others, you'll know why . . . .

(All of the following material was transcribed from a talk which I presented in a workshop recently, without notes, in an informal fashion.)

The historical roots of tantra

There are two main streams of tantra in our heritage — usually called Buddhist Tantra and Hindu Tantra. Most of my education was in Buddhist Tantra, which is more recent and more well-documented than Hindu Tantra. Hindu Tantra is far more ancient than recorded history, and involves the followers of the god Shiva, the Cosmic Dancer, a symbol of the forces of destruction.

The Hindu trinity consists of Brahma the Creator, Vishnu the Sustainer, and Shiva the Destroyer, and all three have their perfect place and time. Hindu Tantra is a beautiful tradition — but for our purposes here I'll concentrate on Buddhist Tantra, which flourished in Tibet until 1959, when China moved in and took control.

For most Tibetans, who are staunch Buddhists, their history really begins with the advent of Buddhism into their country. Before Buddhism, the Tibetans of today often describe themselves as having been a very wild people, even 'blue-faced monkeys' — after the practice they had of painting their faces blue when waging war. They were known as fierce warriors, and they practiced a form of magic which was very powerful — and sometimes very destructive — known as 'Bon' (pronounced *bone*) magic.

By 800 A.D., Buddhism had been growing for 1300 years — the Buddha, Shakyamuni Gautama, taught in India in 500 B.C. In that 1300 years, Buddhism had spread south and east, to Sri Lanka, Burma, Thailand, Indochina and Malaya; it had spread north, to China and Mongolia; and it spread into Japan, where it evolved into Zen. Buddhism covered much of the Eastern world, most of Asia, and it had great impact and popularity in all of the countries which adopted it. But it was unable to penetrate into Tibet, mainly because of the powerful opposition of the Bon religion, and because of the people's inability to understand the principles of the so-called 'religion', or philosophy, or set of teachings leading to liberation which is known as 'Buddhism'.

The king of Tibet in the 8th centruy A.D. is one of the most famous and revered in Tibetan history, because he was the one who initiated the advent of the new religion, the new teachings which transformed the quality of life of all the people in the country. He was named Trison Detsan, and it is said he was an *incarnated* king — in a previous lifetime, he had created enough good karma to be reborn not only as a king, but as someone who was very open to the truth of the *dharma*, the universal teachings of the Buddha.

The king became very deeply influenced by Buddhism and wanted to introduce it into his country. Several well-known and powerful people were brought in from India to do this, including the great saint Shanti Rakshita, but they were all unable to do so. Every time a temple or any other structure was attempted to be built, it would fall, totally destroyed through the efforts of the Bon magicians. There were earthquakes, and lightning, and anything the Buddhists attempted to build was immediately destroyed.

Finally, the king summoned the great magician and mystic and teacher named Padma Sambhava to come to Tibet. Padma Sambhava was born in an ancient land called Urgyan or Uddiyana, which is probably part of present day Nepal. There are many legends surrounding the life and teachings of Padma Sambhava. His name literally means 'Lotus Born', because he is said to not have been born in the usual way, but to have been spontaneously generated by the forces of the divine nature of the universe, as a year-old infant, seated in the center of a huge lotus flower, deep in meditation, with sweat on his brow, in the middle of a sacred lake named Dhanakosha. He was found by some people who took him to the king of the region, and was taken to the palace and brought up to be a king. But he tired of the royal life, and went off in search of the deepest and most profound teachings he could find.

It is said that Padma Sambhava studied with Ananda, the Buddha's favorite disciple, the one with the huge, open heart who remembered all of the Buddha's 84,000 oral teachings or *sutras*. If so, that would make Padma Sambhava 1300 years old, at least by Western reckoning, by the time he came to Tibet. But it is also said that Padma Sambhava had mastered many powers, one of which was the power of immortality.

It is said that, after studying with Ananda and all the great teachers of Buddhism at the time in India, Padma Sambhava wandered through India for many years, having a great number of adventures and spending five years meditating in each of the eight great cemeteries of ancient India. He built houses of bones and lived in them, a freak and a recluse. And it is in those cemeteries that he was given the teachings of tantra, by *dakinis* — women of many different forms who came to him in meditation. He became an adept, then a great master, and his fame spread wide.

And so, the king of Tibet invited this man to come to his country to establish the dharma. Padma Sambhava came, and the king met him on the border of Tibet. Being the king, he of course assumed that this teacher would bow down before him. But Padma Sambhava did not bow down before the king. The king was perplexed, because everyone bowed down before him. The histories say, however, that Padma Sambhava simply raised one finger, and a lightning bolt shot from the tip of it and stopped a very short distance from the king's nose. The king, in awe, fell on his knees in supplication, and became one of Padma Sambhava's most powerful disciples.

The histories of Tibet are colorful, unusual, and amazing. They are unlike the histories of the West in many ways — unless you count the Bible as an historical work. For like the Bible, Tibetan histories are filled with stories which many may reject as being impossible or untrue. I'm simply relating some of the stories I have heard from Tibetans themselves talking of their history, and from several translations of Tibetan books. Accept them or reject them as you will, it doesn't matter. For my part, I think they are wonderful, in the deepest sense of the word — filled with wonder and light and deep teachings for us, if we have ears to hear. I've noticed a tendency in many people to be skeptical when hearing of the miracles that are part of the traditions of other countries — and yet many of these people firmly believe in the miracles of Christ, the Genesis stories of creation and the great flood, Moses turning a stick into a snake and crossing the Red Sea, and so on . . . . So often, we accept the familiar and reject the unfamiliar. But back to our story . . . .

Padma Sambhava went into Tibet, and began building the first Buddhist temple at a place called Samye Ling. He told the king that, in order to do this, he had to first be able to meditate in absolute uninterrupted silence, and he went up into an isolated cave in order to do so, of which only the king himself knew the location.

After a while, a certain man came to the king — a

well-dressed man, very striking. He told the king that he was an important merchant, and that he had a great gift for the king, because he supported him in his efforts to try to establish Buddhism in the country. His gift was a huge amount of red cedar for the building of his temple. Cedar in Tibet is a very rare and precious commodity, because it has to be hauled in through hundreds of rough mountainous miles. The king was overwhelmed at this generous offer. The man said that the king should tell Padma Sambhava about it immediately. The king said he was in meditation and did not want to be disturbed. The man said that he was certain that if Padma Sambhava knew of this gift, he would want to be told about it — he would want his meditation interrupted, because it would fulfill the goals of his meditation.

So the king went up to the cave and entered. In the depths of the cave it is told that he saw, at first, not Padma Sambhava in meditation, but a huge *garuda* bird — a garuda is very much like the thunderbird of the American Indians, a symbol of power and spiritual flight, a huge, strong bird, with powerful arms as well as wings. This bird was devouring a large *naga*, or snake — a symbol of the dark forces which were preventing them from reaching their goals. The garuda had almost entirely devoured the snake — only the tail end was left, dangling from his beak. As soon as the garuda saw the king, the great bird's eyes grew large, and a fierce struggle ensued. The snake gained strength, and was able to release itself from the garuda's massive jaws and get out of the cave with astounding speed. The king could do nothing — even as the snake whipped right past him.

The garuda instantly retransformed back into Padma Sambhava — and he was enraged at the king. He shouted, "Why did you interrupt my meditation?" And the king said that he had been told to talk to him, for a fantastic man had given them a great amount of cedar wood to build their temple.

Padma Sambhava shouted, "Fool!" That man was the king of the nagas, and he did all that in order to trick you into interrupting my meditation. And because you have interrupted it, the nagas have gotten away — and now I'm not able to control their activities."

The king was dismayed — and he must have felt very strange when Padma Sambhava continued with these words:

"In spite of your interruption, I will be able to establish Buddhism in this country. But because of your interruption, at a time in the future, when iron birds shall fly and people will travel in machines with wheels, Buddhism will be driven from your country by armies from the north, and the great teachings will be totally crushed in Tibet, and they will move to the West, to the land of the Red Man."

The king could probably make very little sense of these predictions, for they weren't to come true for another 1150 (or so) years. Saddened and disheartened, he returned home. Padma Sambhava continued his meditation.

Soon they were able to construct the great temple at Samye Ling — the temple which was to be the first to introduce the powerful teachings of Buddhism into Tibet. The king became one of Padma Sambhava's most evolved disciples. Twenty-five other disciples became very famous, as well. A Tibetan woman, named Yeshey Tsogyal, became Padma Sambhava's chief *dakini* and disciple and biographer, and it is said that she was able to understand and transmit all of his teachings, and all of his awareness — something no other disciple accomplished.

The story of Tibetan Buddhism is really the story of Padma Sambhava, because he is the great founder and fountainhead of Buddhism in Tibet. He is revered by the Tibetan people much as Christ is revered in the West. Padma Sambhava is called the father of Buddhist Tantra — and his brilliant contribution to Tibet, and now to the world in general, is his adaptation of the teachings of the Buddha into a form which the people can readily understand and apply in their daily lives.

The original spoken words of Buddha in India, called the *sutras,* are the work of a mind of incredible intellect and power and breadth and depth. His original words were obviously presented to a people who were highly civilized, highly evolved and intelligent. The people of Tibet, however, were wild, relatively uneducated, very physical, emotional, intense, and not at all suited to hear teachings that were so subtle, sublime, and intellectually demanding.

And so the teachings needed to be adapted to the people of Tibet, so that they could hear them. Padma Sambhava had the depth of understanding to be able to translate Buddha's teachings so that the people could grasp them thoroughly. He did this by writing and introducing and practicing the *tantras.* He adapted the *sutras* of Buddha into the *tantras,* which were written and spoken teachings which were highly pragmatic, and physical, and comparatively non-intellectual. The teachings were adapted to meet the needs of the people, just as they're beginning to be adapted into America today, to meet the needs of a very different people, with a very different mentality and culture.

Padma Sambhava's main disciples became known as the "twenty-five great siddhas," because each of them is said to have attained a great power, or *siddhi.* With the assistance of these twenty-five disciples, Padma Sambhava was able to firmly establish the liberating teachings of Buddhism in Tibet, in spite of a great deal of very powerful opposition. The teachings swept across the entire vast country, and had a transformative impact upon the people and their way of life; the country was changed from bottom to top, from the lives of the simplest common people to the entire political structure, through the introduction of a certain set of teachings now known as Buddhist Tantra.

The Nyingma School

Padma Sambhava and his disciples established what later came to be called the *Nyingma* tradition. Nyingma means 'ancient ones' or 'the old school' — it was called the old school only later, of course, after the new schools developed.... For several hundred years, there was basically one school of Buddhism in Tibet. And then, like all human movements, like Christianity in the West, other traditions, other branches formed when very strong, clear leaders came along and adapted or changed the teachings, or generated new teachings based on their own experience and channeling...

The Nyingma, the first school in Tibet, started to become criticized by newly developing schools because they felt — and this is an interesting and recurring pattern — that the Nyingma was too similar to the original Bon magic. The teachings of Buddha originally had to adapt a great deal to penetrate into the country. Once they did successfully adapt, they laid the foundation for other schools to come along and say that they adapted too much, that they were too much like their predecessors. A natural inclination, a natural cycle.

People started saying that the Nyingma was just the Bon ritual in reverse — that their altars and practices were totally similar, except that they mirrored each other, they reversed each other. The Nyingma would always spin their prayer wheels and do their circumambulations (walking in a circle, chanting or meditating) in a clockwise direction, for example, while the Bon magicians would spin their prayer wheels and do their circumambulations in a *counter*clockwise direction. In Nyingma tradition, deities are placed on the altar in a certain arrangement; in Bon tradition, the placement is similar, but reversed.

The Nyingmas, of course, did not agree with their critics and did not change their ways. The tradition continues today, as one of the strongest and most vital of all the schools of Tibetan Buddhism. It is led by a highly revered teacher named Dudjom Rinpoche.

The Gelugpa School

And so, different schools came along — the so-called reformed schools — who felt that the Nyingma had adapted too much to their Bon competitors. The newer schools claimed that they were getting back closer to the original purity of Buddhism in India. One of the most notable of the reformed schools was the *Gelugpa,* which sprang from the teachings of a man named Tsong Kapa, who lived in the 13th century, several hundred years after the Nyingma school was established.

The powerful Gelugpas ended up gaining most of the political control of the country by about 1800 A.D. Tibet's system of government was very unusual; the spiritual leaders were also the political leaders. The head of the Gelugpa sect is the Dalai Lama, and he, during the course of several hundred years and over two dozen incarnations became the political leader of much of Tibet. (Those from Eastern Tibet, like my Nyingma teacher, claimed that they were virtually independent from Gelugpa rule.)

The Gelugpa developed as a very scholarly tradition, very much in contrast to the Nyingma's more pragmatic and practical approach.

The Kargyud School

Another school which developed later was called the *Kargyud* school. The Kargyud in many ways is similar to the Nyingma school, stressing practice and personal experience, rather than intellectual knowledge. The tradition of the Kargyuds came through a different source than the Nyingma. It's a very important tradition, because it is still being carried on in India and in this country today by Chögyam Trungpa and many others.

The Nyingma tradition, as I have said, stems primarily from Padma Sambhava, and claims to go directly back to Shakyamuni Buddha. The Kargyud tradition stems from an original and powerful teacher — a man named Tilopa, who illustrates the essence of tantra.

It all began back in India, probably around 800 A.D. By this time, Buddhism had spread throughout India, and the *Mahayana* — the out-reaching form of Buddhism, the Buddhism of the *Bodhisattva*, the seeker dedicated to helping all beings attain enlightenment — was at its height, in full flower. There were great Buddhist universities throughout India, the greatest of which was

Nalanda University. The most well-known, well-educated and powerful teacher at Nalanda was named Naropa. He had thousands of disciples, and was deeply respected and revered as a great Mahayana Buddhist, a great scholar and teacher.

The histories say that one night Naropa had a dream, and in the dream, a wild, naked old *dakini* (a woman who brings teachings) came to him, dancing wildly, laughing at him, pointing, shrieking, saying, "You think you are such a great scholar! If you wish to know, you will listen to the first name that you hear tomorrow, and you will find that man and learn his teachings. If you don't do this, you will never grow any more! You are stuck in your own pride!"

And she laughed at him wildly. He woke up in a cold sweat, deeply unsettled by his dream. He walked over to his window, and beneath his balcony, he heard three beggars talking, and they mentioned a great yogi named Tilopa. As soon as he heard this name *Tilopa,* a deep feeling flashed through his whole being — yes!, he knew he must find the great yogi Tilopa, whoever he was, because he knew that Tilopa had deep teachings for him, far beyond anything he had ever encountered before. Naropa, a patriarch for thousands, became like a little child that day.

That same day he informed his disciples he was leaving to go in search of his teacher. His disciples were deeply upset, and begged him, pleaded with him to stay and teach, saying that he was their greatest teacher, and how could he leave them, when they needed his guidance and light? But he said that he had to go — and they would find their own way. So, in spite of the desperate supplications of thousands of his students, Naropa wandered off, in search of the great yogi Tilopa.

He covered the entire country, asking everywhere, at every population center, for the great yogi Tilopa. But no one had ever heard of him! He refused to get discouraged, and started asking at the smaller towns and tiniest villages, wandering, canvassing the entire country, searching for the great yogi Tilopa. He continued, asking everyone, everywhere.

Ten years passed — ten years of fruitless wandering. And yet he was undaunted. Twelve years passed. Such was his persistence that he could wander for twelve years, looking for a man no one had ever heard of. Finally, when he was beginning his thirteenth year of wandering, at a very small village on the southern coast of India, as he asked for the great yogi Tilopa, some people laughed and said, "We don't know any great yogi Tilopa, but there's a bum named Tilopa who lives down the beach. He's so lazy, he doesn't do anything but lie around all day. He doesn't work. All he eats are the fish heads that the fishermen throw away."

Naropa went in search of this man, and sure enough, he found an old, grizzled bum lying on the sand. He asked if his name was Tilopa. The man nodded. He asked for his instruction. The man laughed, and kept lying there, half asleep, totally ignoring Naropa. Naropa asked again for his instruction, and got absolutely no reply, and saw nothing but a grizzly old bum asleep in the sand.

For three days, Tilopa just lay there, doing nothing, eating some fish heads now and then, acting as if Naropa was not there at all, totally ignoring him. Finally, at the end of the third day, he turned to Naropa and nodded, saying without a word that he would take him in as a disciple, if he was strong enough, if he was open enough to receive the teachings.

Naropa was slowly whittled down, from being a highly esteemed, respected scholar and teacher to becoming a bum just like Tilopa.

Tilopa would do things like tell Naropa of a wedding feast people were having nearby. He told Naropa to crash the feast, and bring him something for his supper. This was considered extremely unacceptable in ancient India. Nevertheless, Naropa went to the wedding, pretending to be a guest, and got himself a dinner, which he brought to Tilopa, who devoured every bit of it, quickly and greedily. Then he told Naropa that he could go back and get himself a supper — so Naropa went back once again and got himself another meal. But this time they discovered him and said, "You weren't invited to this wedding!" And they beat him within an inch of his life and left him in a ditch. Tilopa found him there, lying in the ditch, bleeding and bruised and dazed, and he simply laughed, and went on his way.

Another time, it is said that they were wandering through the jungle, and came to a little stream, about five feet across. Tilopa said, "Lay down across that stream — I want to walk over your back." So Naropa laid down in the stream, and Tilopa walked over his back, and Naropa got up and found that his body was covered with big, sucking, clinging leeches, for the stream was infested with them. Again, Tilopa simply laughed, as Naropa frantically tore the leeches from his body.

They say that the education of Naropa by Tilopa lasted twelve years. And in that time, no teachings were given — at least nothing that had the usual appearance of some kind of teaching. It was simply a matter of living from day to day.

The histories become even more incredible at this point — more mystical, more miraculous, like the story of Christ healing Lazarus. They even go so far as to say that at one point, they were walking along and came to a high cliff with sharp, jagged rocks several hundred feet below. Tilopa said, "If you have faith in me as your teacher, dive off that cliff!" Naropa took one look at the rocks below . . . and dove . . . . His body smashed into the rocks, and was instantly torn into bleeding shreds . . . . Then Tilopa started demonstrating some of his powers — for he sat cross-legged at the top of the cliff and did a powerful chant (or *mantra*), which pulled the mutilated pieces of Naropa's body back together. Naropa gained consciousness . . . and was alive, and well . . . .

One day Tilopa turned and looked deeply at Naropa, staring into his eyes for a long, long time . . . . Naropa was now a very different person than the one who came to him twelve years ago — his pride was gone, his arrogance was gone, his role-playing as a scholar and a teacher was gone . . . . He was open, open like a child . . . .

Yet one last step was needed, because Tilopa took off his shoe, his beat-up sandal, and turned and without one word of warning smashed Naropa in the face very hard with the sole of his sandal. Naropa's mind suffered a shock . . . and the aftermath of that shock propelled him into a great space, a light he'd never imagined before, never known before, never experienced before.

After a moment, Tilopa told him, "Now you are ready — now you are ready for the great teachings of the *Mahamudra*." With that, Tilopa passed on all the teachings of the lineage to Naropa — teachings which he had received from teachers beyond the physical plane, in direct spiritual transmission. For it is taught that Tilopa himself got the teachings from celestial sources, from no one incarnated in a physical body, but rather from the great teachers of Buddha and Christ and everyone who has deep understanding gained from sources other than teachers who walk this earth.

Tilopa gave the great teachings of the *Mahamudra* to Naropa. Mahamudra literally means "the great gesture," and it embodies a number of teachings which have been recorded and translated today, and serve as a cornerstone of much of Buddhist tantra.

Naropa's greatest disciple was a Tibetan named Marpa, who made the perilous journey from Tibet to India three times, bringing with him great offerings of gold to Naropa. Naropa passed on the teachings of the Mahamudra to Marpa, who became known as the Translator, for he adapted many of the teachings for the Tibetan people.

Marpa the Translator's greatest disciple was a skinny little yogi named Milarepa, who became famous for his songs and his divine ecstatic vision . . . and for his simple, austere life and his great yogic power . . . . And through the lineage of Tilopa, Naropa, Marpa, and Milarepa came the great school of the Kargyud. It is very close to the Nyingma in many ways — in fact, many of the great teachers studied with both schools.

Today, eight branches of the Kargyud exist. One of the most important of these branches is the *Karma Kargyud*, which is led by the famous Karmapa, who is the seer, the visionary leader — or at least consultant — for all of the schools.

The incarnation of the Karmapa is still a very strong leader today. He often tours, performing *pujas* — ritual ceremonies — such as the 'Black Hat' ceremony, which is his specialty, and can assist people in finding their own personal empowerment.

The Sakya School

Four great schools developed in Tibet, and grew strong and prospered, until well into the middle of the 20th century. The other prominent school which developed is the *Sakya* school. Its traditions are much like the Nyingma. Originally, most Nyingmas were located east of Lhasa, while the Sakyas were located west of Lhasa. Most were farmers; many lived close to the Nepal border, where they easily escaped the Chinese invasion. They now align themselves with the Nyingma and Kargyud.

A story...

There was, and still is, rivalry among the different schools, of course, but many students and many of the great teachers, the great *lamas*, studied in several schools, and taught students of different schools. It was not nearly so separate as our Christian churches tend to be.

And in many ways, it wasn't so serious as many branches of Western religion have become. As Tibetan Buddhism grew to embrace the whole culture, it reflected the joy and spontaneity and freedom of a truly unique people. When I was studying with Lama Tarthang Tulku, in Berkeley, we would often try, especially in our intense and demanding language classes, to get him off the subject of language and into the many stories he had from his childhood in Tibet. Fascinating, wonderful stories. Perhaps this one story will give you a better glimpse of Tibetan history than you'll get from a great many books — this is a story the Lama told us in a language class.

It seems that there are a whole series of jokes and stories about a certain wandering Nyingma yogi in ancient Tibet. The stories are very much like our 'traveling salesman' jokes — only they're 'wandering yogi' jokes. Some of them are explicitly, uninhibitedly sexual. Here's one that's quite different. (If any of the language or concepts in it seems offensive to you, that's good! Look at it as an opportunity to really *see* the things you reject, and see if they're worth bothering about, and see if you're a freer person if you just let them go.)

Once upon a time, many years ago, in a huge valley in Tibet, the people and animals and plants suffered a terrible drought. There was no rain for weeks and weeks during the warmest summer months, and crops were drying up, and the animals were suffering. A thousand Gelugpa monks gathered on the floor of the valley and chanted for rain. They chanted for ten days and ten nights — and yet the skies remained deep blue and dry.

Then, a certain wandering Nyingma yogi came up to the monks. He looked at them and laughed. He was wearing a tattered *Chuba* (or robe), tied at the waist. He climbed a tree, in front of them, and hung by his knees, upside down. His robe fell over his head, exposing his bare ass hanging in the tree. He let loose a loud fart which resounded through the valley . . . and suddenly the sky was filled with huge, billowing rain clouds rushing over the valley, and they were drenched in a warm wondrous shower, which soaked the parched earth, and turned it from brown to green and yellow and red and orange and all the colors of all the flowers and plants of the world.

And he ran away, laughing, yelling out to them, so that all could hear, "See! One Nyingma fart is worth 10,000 Gelugpa chants!"

This history is brief and unscholarly. There is much more that could be said. But history is important only in ways in which it reflects and affects us here and now. So we'll move on . . .

Tibetan Buddhism today

In 1959, Padma Sambhava's predictions came true. The government to the north of Tibet, isolated from them by the great wall of the Himalayan mountains, had been very aggressive for thousands of years. In 1959, armies marched in from the north and blatantly took over Tibet — an imperialistic move, a move which will have karmic results for the 'People's Republic of China', just as America's and Russia's imperialism is faced with their own karmic results. For you simply can't just move into another country and take it over by physical power, without suffering deep karmic results that will someday balance the scales of justice. "As you sow, so shall you reap." China took over Tibet, forcefully drove out Buddhism, and forcefully — against a great amount of resistance from the Tibetan people — implanted China's new teachings, the teachings of Chairman Mao, which has led to physical power overcoming spiritual power — for the moment. China may one day suffer for her aggression. It remains to be seen how.

In one way, these very unfortunate circumstances for Tibet were fortunate for the West, because they forced many lamas, including Chögyam Trungpa, Tarthang Tulku, Dudjom Rinpoche, the Dalai Lama, the Karmapa and many others (representing all four schools), out of Tibet. And their teachings are beginning to be adapted to a very strange new land: America (and Canada, and Western Europe). America, compared to

Tibet, is extremely violent and ignorant — unaware of the law of karma, unaware of the means to attain true personal freedom. But America's visionary constitutional policy of freedom of religion makes it one of the most fertile and open countries on earth. And so it is in America that the ancient teachings of Tibetan tantra are blossoming, in many new forms — some very traditional, some completely transformed into the new cultural context. American tantra is being born as Buddhist tantra is driven from its homeland.

What exactly do we mean when we say *Buddhist Tantra*? The tantra is a vast body of written and spoken teachings, most of which spring either directly or indirectly from Padma Sambhava. They teach that there are nine levels of Buddhism, nine levels of the teachings of the *dharma*, the truth. The first level is called the *hinayana* (or Theravadan), the so-called "smaller vehicle." This is the teaching that the Tibetan sources say is very self-centered, because it is focused simply on the personal salvation of the aspirant.

The next two of the nine stages are the *mahayana*, or the "great vehicle," which is focused on transformation and enlightenment for all of mankind, in fact for every animal and plant on the planet. The Mahayana is the path of the Bodhisattva, who takes a vow not to attain final enlightenment until every animal and plant and person on this planet has attained enlightenment.

The six paths beyond the Mahayana are called the *vajrayana*, or the "diamond vehicle," or Buddhist tantra. The six levels evolve first in outer, then inner, then secret stages. The first two levels, the first practices, are the *outer* Vajrayana — involving practices which are done on an outer, obvious level, which other people can see. Robes are often worn, and there is public show of the practices, such as public prayer or preaching and so on. It is obvious to all that the person is doing these practices.

The *inner* level, however — the next two stages of the Vajrayana — gives us a set of higher teachings and finer practices which are not necessarily reflected on the outer level. The practices are done in an internal way. Anyone can do these practices, without having to adapt a certain lifestyle, for the practices have become deeply internalized.

Then the deepest levels, the *secret* levels, unfold — the highest levels of the Vajrayana. Here the practices take place on a deep, subtle level which is even beyond the inner level. By "secret," Tibetan teachers always say that they are not intentionally trying to keep secrets from anyone, but that the content of the teachings by their very nature is "self-secret" — they simply cannot be communicated in spoken or written words . . . they cannot be taught, they must be caught, directly, intuitively.

They say that the highest level of Buddhist tantra, the ninth level of their practical philosophy and spiritual cosmology is called the *Dzog Chen,* or the level of "absolute perfection." This is the highest level of awareness possible, which sees the total perfection in every level of the teachings, in every level of our understanding, from ignorance to bliss. This is the path which embraces *all* the teachings, all the ways of life, which sees that every person has their own path, their own understanding and karma, and that it is perfect for every person on every level to be exactly where they are . . . . So the highest Buddhist tantra embraces even the *hinayana,* embraces everything and everyone, and every way of life. The greatest teaching of Buddhist tantra is the perfection of all paths. It is perfect for you to be doing exactly what you are doing at this moment.

Tantra in the West

Tantra is vital and relevant to the West today, because of its adaptability. Infinite creativity is encouraged. The teachings of Buddha — outer, inner, and secret — went through a complete metamorphosis in the hands of Padma Sambhava, so that he could present them in a form which the wild, warlike Tibetans could understand. Once again, the teachings of both Buddha and Padma Sambhava (and Christ, and Krishna, and Shiva, and the Native Americans, and every sane culture that has ever lived) are being totally changed, transformed, to adapt to a wild and even sometimes warlike new culture which we call the West. But the essence of the teaching — the shimmering, wonderful essence of all spiritual truths of all cultures — remains the same. And by discovering it, we can be free, totally free, in every way we want to be. And by applying our discoveries, we can change our nation, and eventually change our world, into a place which respects human life, and which respects all life, and which will never again fight wars of violence and destruction in order to achieve political and material things which we don't really need for our happiness or freedom.

The teachings of the Buddhist tantra have come to the West. And many other similar teachings are emerging, from both Eastern and Western sources (such as the Dead Sea Scrolls, which are giving us many of the Essene and Gnostic works which were edited out of the Bible by arch-Conservatives hundreds of years after Christ). And they show us that *we* have the teachings, the answers, the way to complete freedom deep within our own hearts, deep within our cultural heritage.

I'd like to close by giving you one of those deepest secret teachings, which must be experienced, not

merely understood intellectually. And if it is grasped,
nothing more need be understood:

> *The kingdom of heaven*
> *is within*

So be it. So it is!

Appendix B

Reflections

The following are a series of miscellaneous reflections, to be read at random. Some are traditional teachings, some are not. Give each one its own moment.

———————————

Slow down as you read this.... Just take a few of the words, and sit with them, absorb them. Give yourself the gift of silence, occasionally — even if it seems that nothing at all is happening... rest assured that something *is* happening. Let whatever happens happen... without expectations.

Let there be silence.... Within it is some deep truth for you....

———————————

The most important thing is just to relax... to go within occasionally and not try to *make* anything happen.

We're not trying to describe any kind of particular experience — we're just assisting people (including ourselves) to open the doors into the infinite number of creative experiences within us all . . . .

The truth is within you.

So many people who become teachers and/or writers have had a legitimate, beautiful experience which they are trying to express and give to other people.

But so often their teachings, organizations, systems, etc., become imbued with the idea that you have to do it *their* way — the way the original teacher did it . . . when in fact there are an infinite number of ways to do it, each tailored to a different individual.

All we 'teach' are the infinite ways . . . . All we do is encourage people to look within, and find their own path, their own answers in their hearts . . . .

Things unfold in this practice differently for everyone. Everyone will not have the same experiences at all — yours will be unique, in many vital, beautiful ways.

The first teaching of the Medicine Wheel of the Native Americans, which is so similar to the teachings of Tibetan Buddhism (and so clearly and beautifully expressed in the book, *Seven Arrows*), is that *no two people see the same thing* . . . . Everyone has their own unique perspective, their own way of living and seeing and growing.

Relax . . . and look within. The answers you find there are perfect for you.

What is tantra?

It comes from the Sanskrit root word meaning *to weave* . . . .

> '*O, what a tangled web we weave...*'
> (Sir Walter Scott,
> *Marmion*, Canto vi)

Our purpose on earth in physical bodies is to fulfill the activity of being, to realize our highest dreams . . . .

Here is a practice of tantra:

> *Look at what you find yourself disliking* . . .
> *Look at your body aging* . . .
> *Look at old age* . . .
> *Look at sickness* . . .
> *Look at death* . . .
> *Look at insanity* . . .
> *Look at anything and everything you reject* . . .
> *And find the beauty in it* . . .
> *And see the perfection of it all.*

Let the world become a beautiful place for you — in spite of so many apparent imperfections. Let go of how you think it *should be* . . . and see the beauty and perfection of *what is* . . . here and now, totally complete, totally perfect.

Every birth, every death, every accident, *everything* is totally as it should be . . . . How could it be any other way?

Look at the perfection of our galaxies, our solar system, our earth, and our bodies . . . .

We are perfect beings.

Let your true inner beauty shine forth.

This is the highest teaching of tantra.

Find a picture ... or an object ... or a phrase ... or whatever — find something that reminds you of what you know — and carry it with you.

A treasure map ... a jewel ... a picture of someone showering you with love from their eyes ... a prayer, a song, a musical instrument ... whatever resonates with you.

And carry it with you, in your heart.

It is your reminder that all is perfect ... there's nothing to worry about ... the Universe provides for you ... God is love.

Say it in whatever way you will ....

Aleister Crowley wrote a very insightful book called *Yoga*. In one passage he says something worth repeating, regarding this book, or any other book or teacher:

> *"Only 90 or 95 percent of these words are the ravings of a disordered mind — the rest is pure gold."*
> (This is somewhat paraphrased)

Take the words here that really resonate with you, and take them to heart ... and let all the other words go, as you let everything else go .... Let it be.

To each their own.

I must speak my deepest, most honest thoughts about many of the Eastern teachings (and Western too, for that matter) that are becoming popular in America and other parts of the West today ....

I remember, through so many periods of my studies of Eastern practices and philosophies, going through a deep rejection of almost everything from my past, and from my culture and heritage in general.

I remember one night, when I was deeply into my studies of Tibetan Buddhism, taking a walk through the campus of the University in Berkeley ... then I strolled up Telegraph Avenue, then up the hill past the fraternities and sororities, toward the place I lived, the Tibetan Meditation Center ....

As I approached the Meditation Center, wandering somewhat aimlessly, thinking many thoughts, in no particular hurry to be anywhere, a very clear voice suddenly spoke to me from within. It had a confident, forceful quality — a quality I've grown to understand and trust, for it is one of those moments when I connect with my intuitive teacher, and the truth springs forth, loud and clear. The voice said, *"Look at yourself! Look at what you've been doing: when you went through the campus your mind was filled with thoughts of rejection, putting all the students down for their academic lives, and for being constantly in their heads, their rational minds, and cutting off their emotions and their experience... and when you went up Telegraph Avenue, you were rejecting the people on the street for being violent and stupid derelicts... and when you went by the fraternities, you were rejecting those people for being ignorant sheep, stupid racist macho drunkards... and when you went by the sororities, you rejected those women for being sheltered and sheepish and living in the past.... Everyone you have encountered you have rejected! Is this what you want the result of your education to be?"*

And I realized that as long as I'm rejecting so many things in my world which I'm encountering, I'm not free! True freedom consists of being able to do anything, go anywhere, with anyone, and find value in it, and appreciate and enjoy the people involved.

That moment in my life was a turning point for me, for it forced me to start looking at the attitudes which these Eastern teachings were fostering in me, and in the others who were involved in similar kinds of study. It wasn't easy for me, but I finally had to admit that many of those teachings were creating as many neuroses as they were dissolving. And I finally had to leave, and go elsewhere for other teachings that would open me up more to others, rather than cut me off with a wall of rejection. I searched for, and found, teachings that were better adapted to the West. This book is my attempt to share those teachings with you.

Living sanely and happily and comfortably is all just a matter of balance: On the one hand, take the time and energy to express your feelings and desires as clearly and directly as possible. You can have exactly what you want, if you but visualize your wishes clearly and consistently, and express yourself directly.

On the other hand, however, accept whatever happens, with as few expectations as possible: It's all happening for a very good reason, whether or not it's apparent at the time.

Here's a deep, ancient truth which every child knows:

Row, row, row your boat
Gently down the stream

> *Merrily*
> *Merrily*
> *Merrily*
> *Merrily*
> *Life is but a dream*

This is somewhat repetitious, but it's worth repeating. Tibetan Buddhism — and many other sources of knowledge — say that reality can be perceived on three levels: outer, inner, and 'secret'.

The *outer* plane is the physical plane — that which appears to the five outer senses, material, concrete rewlity.

The *inner* plane is the visionary plane, perceived by the finer senses of our inner vision, our intuition, our imagination, our dreams . . . . This is the so-called 'astral plane', the plane on which magic occurs, the plane of mental creation which precedes physical creation.

The *secret* plane is even beyond this. It is the highest spiritual plane . . . where it is all One . . . where we are all One . . . we are it . . . it is us . . . beyond words. It is called 'secret' only because it can't be really explained in words — not because anyone is trying to keep it secret. It is 'self-secret', because it must be grasped in a very subtle way, beyond our usual methods of learning and even perceiving.

A visionary is a person who sees on the inner and secret planes, as well as the outer plane . . . .

The highest path of Tantric Buddhism is called "Dzog Chen" or "Absolute Perfection." For one who practices it, there are no special outer rituals, there are not necessarily even any inner practices . . . . The only focus is upon the innermost, the 'secret': seeing the total perfection of what is, the perfection of every moment.

It may take a broader perspective than you are now aware of, but these words are true: every moment of your life has been absolutely perfect. And it will continue to be so.

And it is true for everyone else as well . . . .

To quote a great teacher of "Dzog Chen" named Long Chen Pa, who lived seven hundred years ago:

> *"Since everything is but an apparition,*
> *perfect in being what it is, having nothing to*
> *do with good or bad, acceptance or rejection,*
> *one may well burst out in laughter."*

A deep truth, expressed by John Lilly:

We can create whatever space we wish, in our creative imaginations. Once we imagine any space, once we envision it, we can move into that space.

Any barriers to this process can be dissolved with repeated imagining, and with other skillful means (see John Lilly's book, *The Center of the Cyclone,* and Shakti Gawain's book, *Creative Visualization,* for an elaboration of this teaching).

Here is a deep teaching of tantra, and of the Kabbala (Jewish mysticism, one of the main roots of Western magic), and of the Native Americans, and of many other sources:

We are multi-dimensional beings . . . we have different levels of being, which can be called "bodies." We function on four different levels, simultaneously: the physical, the emotional, the mental, and the spiritual. We have a physical body, emotions, thoughts, and a spirit. As we move from the physical to the spiritual, each level of being, each body, becomes finer and even, in a sense, larger — it encompasses more space and more awareness.

Some people are focusing purely on their physical level of being. Their continual focus is upon their body, or others' bodies — their strength, or weakness, their aches and pains, their needs, their health, the perfect diet, the latest techniques for healthful living, their looks, their lovers, their attractiveness or unattractiveness, their operations, their hernia, their digestion, their tension, etc., etc. They eat too much, or they don't eat enough, with a neurotic need to be skinny and fashionable.

I don't mean to reject the physical plane in any way — it is beautiful, it is a key to the infinite . . . it is pleasurable, it is perfect. But focusing *solely* on the physical plane (or solely on any plane, for that matter), is excessive and leads to a narrow view of reality.

Some people are focusing almost exclusively on their emotional level of being. They are deeply involved in their personal dramas, their highs and their lows . . . their feelings have complete control over their behavior. Their continual focus is upon their feelings, or on others' feelings — whether they're comfortable, or upset, or feeling guilty, or feeling high and clear, whether their heart is open, or whether they're feeling uptight.... They may drink too much, or take any number of drugs in order to alter their feelings or even obliterate them so that they don't have to deal with them. Or they may be excessively moderate and rigid, not allowing themselves to do a great number of spontaneous things. They may have deeply repressed feelings of anger or hostility that they would never allow themselves to express, so they create a tension in their body that drives them to escapism and/or excess in many forms, such as food, movies, drugs, alcohol, and even a wide variety of physical and emotional diseases.

This is not to reject the emotional plane in any way (or drugs or alcohol or food or movies either — for they can all be used skillfully and pleasurably). Our emotions are beautiful, and they are a key to the infinite. Our emotions are the key to our intuitive teacher, and our psychic senses, and they are perfect. But focusing only on the emotional plane, like any other, is excessive and limited.

Some people are focusing purely on their mental level of being. The ideas of their minds are the only things worthwhile. Many of these people are in the universities and in the sciences. Their continual focus is upon their own or others' brilliant scholarship or ideas; they're either talking about recent books they have read, or someone's theories, or perhaps someone's neuroses or stupidity or brilliance. They may be completely out of touch with their physical or emotional or spiritual bodies, lost in their mental life. They may feel that the scientific method — a purely rational devise — is the only valid basis for any belief, and they may totally reject anything that has to do with the intuitive or psychic (and which comes through emotional and spiritual bodies), such as spiritual healing or psychic powers or creative visualization or true magic.

This is not to reject the mental plane in any way: it is a fantastically powerful tool . . . it is very useful and expansive . . . it is perfect. But focusing purely on the mental plane ignores too many other phases of existence.

There are even some people who focus purely on the spiritual level of being. This is not too common in mainstream America, but the so-called *spiritual* scene has many of them. Their continual focus is upon their spiritual development, or the level of achievement of their teachers or gurus, or the level of their friends' or other people's spiritual awareness. Many of them reject a great deal of the material universe, including a great deal of our environment and culture. Many of them reject physical, emotional, and sometimes even mental ways of being altogether; some of them reject relating to each other.

Every level of being has its own truth and power and perfection . . . yet every level has its own neuroses, if they aren't balanced with an awareness of the other levels. For every level of the divine tree of life — the structure of the universe in the words of the Kabbala — is perfect. We are physical, emotional, mental, and spiritual beings. We are all of it.

Embrace all of yourself, without rejecting any part of yourself. Don't reject your body, your emotions, your mind, or your spirit.

Look at the Tarot card of the magician — and see that it is you . . . . Everyone is a magician, a creator . . . channeling the energy of the Universe into the creation of whatever he or she chooses.

THE MAGICIAN.

We have within us the magical implements to create whatever we wish — the wand of the creative mind, the sword of our personal power, the cup of inspiration, and the pentacle of abundance and magic.

All of these tools are within us, waiting to be used . . . . All of the higher forces of the universe are at hand, waiting to be called.

Ask, and you shall receive, seek and you will find, knock and the door will be opened unto you . . . .

A deep teaching:

Realize your own power. Grasp your own inner worth and vision and insight and dreams . . . and realize that you have the ability to manifest these things.

Most of us, for a great many unclear reasons, gave away the natural power and vision we had as children. We gave it away to Mommy and Daddy . . . we gave it to our friends. And what they thought, what they felt became very important to us.

We gave it to our teachers, and felt we knew nothing.

Now is the time to take it back. Trust yourself. Trust your feelings, always.

Let us take a journey now, you and I . . . . Together we can travel a great distance — much farther than mere miles on this planet, much farther than the stars . . . .

For this journey is within the realm of the mind . . . . And this realm of our mind encompasses all of space, all of the universe . . . .

And every imagined limitation of time and space dissolves as we open the doors to this realm of the mind.

How do we open these doors?

Simply relax . . . trust yourself . . . .

Relax, take three deep breaths, and let yourself sink deep within . . . .

Relax, and let yourself be . . . let yourself drift into

an infinite awareness which encompasses everything... an infinite awareness which you can direct
anywhere you wish in your creative imagination.
   You take it from here....

You can create
whatever your heart desires!

So be it... so it is!

Acknowledgements

This book has been the result of many different people's contributions, ideas, and honest feedback. I'll try to list most of them, even though I'm sure there's some I have omitted.

In general, I would like to acknowledge my close circle of friends and co-workers for their support, insight, and honesty: Shakti Gawain, Jon Bernoff, Rainbow Canyon, Dean Campbell, and Bobbin Zahner — thanks for everything. And thanks to Shakti and Jon and Rainbow and Chi-uh Gawain and Kathryn Hall for reading the manuscript in its various stages, and giving me very helpful feedback. Special thanks must go to Paul Clemens for his excellent job of editing. His comments and contributions were invaluable. Without everyone I have mentioned, this book would be in a very different form, one which would be a lot less understandable and acceptable for many people. Last, but certainly not least, I would like to deeply thank Sharon Scandur for her love and support — and mostly for the joy she finds in so many moments of her life. She doesn't need this book — she's found her freedom already, mostly by riding horses, living in the country, and reading Bartlett's *Familiar Quotations*.

Chapter II

— My definition of tantra was gathered from several sources, mostly Tibetan Buddhist. The final synthesis is my own.

— The story called 'Three different paths' was told to me by Lama Tarthang Tulku, in Berkeley, California.

— Many of the ideas and practices in the section 'Confronting negative feelings' are from Shakti Gawain, author of *Creative Visualization*. This area is definitely a specialty of hers. The technique of shouting in the car when driving alone to release anger was suggested by Pamela Whitney. Yelling at a pillow is a well-known Gestalt technique.

— The four-step exercise in 'A tantric practice' was taught to me by Shakti Gawain, who was given it in a workshop led by Edward O'Hara in Marin County, California.

Chapter III

— I first learned about affirmations from Catherine Ponder, author and Unity Church minister.

— Many of the ideas in 'The act of creation' section are from Israel Regardie, author of *The Tree of Life, The Art of True Healing,* and many other fine books.

— Many of the ideas in the 'Writing affirmations' section came from Shakti Gawain, who got them from Sondra Ray. Her book *I Deserve Love* describes the technique. Shakti's book, *Creative Visualization*, is excellent for affirmations and a lot of other techniques. It was Marc Reymont, head of the New Age Awareness Foundation in San Mateo, California, who first told me the somewhat startling statement that you should be able to achieve results with any affirmation within 21 days.

Chapter IV

— I want to acknowledge Shakti Gawain's clarity and leadership in opening my eyes to the value of communicating in relationship. In her workshops, her private consulting practice and, most of all, in day-to-day contact with her, I have grown a great deal.

— Shakti's mother, Elizabeth ('Chi-uh') Gawain, contributed the second paragraph in the 'What do you want?' section.

— Shirley Luthman gave us the four possible reactions to feedback in the section titled 'The outer plane'. She is a fine author (see Bibliography), and teaches an excellent weekly class in Tiburon, California.

— The ideas in the 'Negotiation' section came from Carey Yuki Hasegawa and Bonnie Sita, during a workshop they led in Berkeley. Carey Yuki has very effectively adapted many of the teachings of Scientology, and uses them in his private practice as a "Bio-feedback clearing consultant."

Chapter VII

— 'Your ideal scene' is an exercise both Shakti Gawain and I have done in our workshops — as are a great many of the other exercises in this book.

— Listing your purpose, then goals, then steps necessary to reach those goals is a technique we learned from Carey Yuki Hasegawa.

— Chi-uh Gawain contributed the first paragraph in the 'Enjoy your work' section at the end of the chapter.

Chapter VIII

—This opening exercise (page 101) was also from Carey Yuki Hasegawa, in a workshop he led in Berkeley, California.

— The 'Creative meditation for money' is my own very free adaptation of Israel Regardie's meditations in his excellent book, *The Art of True Healing*.

— The first encounter I ever had with 'The ten-percent plan' was in a prosperity workshop conducted by Leonard Orr in San Francisco.

Chapter IX

— It was Ken Keyes Jr., author of *Handbook to Higher Consciousness*, who told me the story of being tucked into bed at night in the 'Let go of the judge' section.

— John Donahue is Director of the Minneapolis Institute of Arts Children's Theater.

Chapter X

—The translation of the verse from the 'Shodoka' in the beginning of the chapter was given to me by Robert Aitkin

Roshi at the Maui Zendo, Maui, Hawaii. He co-translated, along with Eido Shimano Roshi. It is reprinted through Robert Aitkin's kind permission.

Chapter XI

— In the section titled 'The silence', the Tibetan approach came from Lama Tarthang Tulku, in Berkeley, California; the traditional Buddhist meditation was given to me by Chi-uh Gawain.

— In the 'Pillar of light' section, I discovered the technique of 'grounding' at the Berkeley Psychic Institute, and through a teacher named David Lovegarden; I learned the technique of sending a healing from Dr. Mildred Jackson, N.D. (Doctor of Naturopathic Medicine), author of *The Handbook of Alternatives to Chemical Medicine*, and the greatest healer I know. She teaches a class every Thursday night at her home in north Berkeley.

— The exercise 'Opening up your energy centers' was given to me by Jon Bernoff. He got it from Ram Dass, during a retreat at the Lama Foundation in Taos, New Mexico.

— The relaxation technique in the 'Creative meditations' section comes from Silva Mind Control. The courses are taught nationally, and they are excellent. There is also a very good book on it by the founder, Jose Silva (see Bibliography).

— Tarthang Tulku Rinpoche of Berkeley, California, taught me about our 'three bodies' in 'A meditation on our three bodies'. I studied 'Kum Nye' from him, also, at the Nyingma Meditation Center in Berkeley. Paul Clemens, my editor and 'dharma brother', added the bit about rubbing the earlobes. He speaks from experience when he says it's good for children — he has five of them.

— The exercise called 'Closing the gates' was given to me by my first teacher of yoga and Indian philosophy, Professor Arya of Minneapolis, Minnesota.

— The last chant under the title 'Mantra' is freely adapted from a prayer of protection given by Catherine Ponder in one of her books.

Chapter XII

— The pattern of running energy in 'Create a young, beautiful body' was adapted from *The Art of True Healing* by Israel Regardie.

— Many of the ideas in 'The principles of healing' section were influenced by Mildred Jackson, N.D.

Chapter XIV

— Tarthang Tulku told me the story of the woman losing her head in a dream.

Appendix A

— Much of this material came from Tarthang Tulku's stories. Other material came from various books, such as Yeshey Tsogyal's biography of Padma Sambhava which is included in *The Tibetan Book of the Great Liberation* translated by Evans-Wentz and published by Oxford.

Bibliography

Highly recommended
—*Creative Visualization* by Shakti Gawain (Whatever Publishing)
—*Reunion: Tools for Transformation* by Marcus Allen, Shakti Gawain, and Jon Bernoff (Whatever Publishing)
— *The Art of True Healing* by Israel Regardie (Helios in England, Samuel Weiser in USA; it is out of print now, but is included in a greater work, *Foundations of Magic*, published by Thorsen in England)
—*Seven Arrows* by Hyemeyohsts Storm (Harper & Row)

Also recommended
— *Gesture of Balance* and *Openness Mind* by Tarthang Tulku, Rinpoche (Dharma Press)
— *Pray and Grow Rich* by Catherine Ponder (Parker Publishing); other good books by her include *The Prospering Power of Love, The Dynamic Laws of Healing,* and *The Dynamic Laws of Prosperity* (all Parker Publishing).
— *The Tree of Life* by Israel Regardie (Weiser)
— *I Deserve Love* by Sondra Ray (Les Femmes)
— *Collections 1979* and *Intimacy: The Essence of Male and*

231

Female by Shirley Luthman (Mehetabel & Co.)

— *Handbook to Higher Consciousness* by Ken Keyes Jr. (Cornucopia Publications)

— *Zen Training* by Katsuki Sekida (Weatherhill)

— *Muddling Toward Frugality* by Warren Johnson (Shambhala)

— *When I Say No, I Feel Guilty* by Manuel J. Smith (Dial Press; Bantam)

— *Meditation in Action* by Chögyam Trungpa (Shambhala); other fine books of his include *Cutting Through Spiritual Materialism* and *Born in Tibet* (also Shambhala)

— *Jonathan Livingston Seagull* and *Illusions* by Richard Bach (Macmillan and Delacorte, respectively)

— *Three Pillars of Zen* by Phillip Kapleau (may be out of print)

— *Varieties of Religious Experience* by William James (Doubleday)

— *Attaining Financial Peace of Mind* by Jack and Lois Johnstad (Bright Spirit Press)

— *Walden* by Henry David Thoreau (Rinehart Editions)

— *The Handbook of Alternatives to Chemical Medicine* by Mildred Jackson, N.D. (Lawton-Teague Publications)

— *Silva Mind Control* by Jose Silva (Simon & Schuster)

— *The Center of the Cyclone* by John C. Lilly, M.D. (Julian Press and Bantam)

— *As A Man Thinketh* by James Allen (DeVorss)

— *The Way of Life* (or *Tao Te Ching*) by Lao Tzu. One of the better translations is by Gia-Fu Feng and Jane English (Vintage)

— *Chrysalis — A journey into the new spiritual America* by Mark Allen (Ross Books)

— *Seeds to the Wind — Poems, Songs, Meditations* by Mark Allen (Whatever Publishing)

Books

Living in the Light by Shakti Gawain. Shows us a new way of life — becoming a channel for the creative power of the Universe by developing our intuition. Offers both practical and inspirational guidance in expanding our perspective on who we are and what we have the potential to become.

Creative Visualization by Shakti Gawain. This clear and practical guide contains easy-to-use techniques to: feel more relaxed and peaceful, increase your vitality and improve your health, develop your creative talents, create more fulfillment in relationships, reach your career goals, dissolve negative habit patterns, increase your prosperity, and much, much more.

Work With Passion—*How To Do What You Love For A Living* by Nancy Anderson. This highly effective guide will help you master the secrets of finding your niche in life — doing what you love to do and getting paid well for it. *Work With Passion* is filled with inspiring stories of ordinary people who have achieved extraordinary results by following the nine-step program of the author, developed during her years as a highly successful career consultant. This is *the* career book of the 1980's!

Friends and Lovers—*How to Create the Relationships You Want* by Marc Allen. An upbeat, knowledgeable, and contemporary guide to living and working with people. Contains a six-step process that is *guaranteed to settle arguments* at home or at work.

Anybody Can Write— *A Playful Approach* by Jean Bryant. A delightful, humorous, and *effective* new book for non-writers, beginners, and writers who are "blocked." It will inspire you to learn to "fingerpaint with words," and encourage you to experience the pleasure and fulfillment of writing.

Cassettes

Creative Visualization. Shakti Gawain guides you through some of the most powerful and effective meditations and techniques from her book. An inspirational cassette.

Living in the Light. In this exciting hour-long interview, Shakti Gawain reveals the main principles and techniques from her book of the same title, showing us how to connect with our intuition and become a creative channel for personal and planetary transformation.

Stress Reduction and Creative Meditations. Marc Allen guides you through a deeply relaxing, stress-reducing experience on the first side. Side Two contains effective, creative meditations for health, abundance, and fulfilling relationships. Soothing background music by Jon Bernoff.

Friends and Lovers—How to Create the Relationships You Want. In this dynamic cassette companion to his book, Marc Allen gives an interview highlighting the most important ideas and techniques from *Friends and Lovers.* Inner work and core beliefs are stressed.

Anybody Can Write. Jean Bryant highlights some of the writing techniques and ideas from her book: trusting yourself, writing without thinking, escape writing, writing with passion, fingerpainting with words.

ORDERING INFORMATION

We invite you to send for a free copy of our full-color catalogue so that you can see our complete selection of books and cassettes.

Whatever Publishing, Inc.
P.O. Box 13257, Northgate Station
San Rafael, CA 94913
(415) 472-2100

ORDER TOLL FREE WITH YOUR VISA/MC
(800) 227-3900
(800) 632-2122 in California

About the Author

Marcus Allen graduated Phi Beta Kappa from the University of Minnesota in 1968. He toured the country, from New York to California, with a professional theater company, the Firehouse Theater. Then he plunged full time into the studies which have culminated in this book: he spent a year studying yoga and Eastern philosophy, two years studying Zen Buddhism, and over three years studying Tibetan ('Tantric') Buddhism at the Nyingma Meditation Center in Berkeley, California.

Over the past five years he has written five books and composed and produced four albums of music. He lives in Marin County, California.

By the Author

Books
> Friends and Lovers—How to Create the
>   Relationships You Want
> Reunion—Tools for Transformation
> Astrology for the New Age—An Intuitive
>   Approach
> Seeds to the Wind—Poems, Songs, Meditations
> Chrysalis

Cassette Tapes
> Stress Reduction and Creative Meditations